Taking Charge

Taking Charge

Your life patterns and their meaning

Gudrun Burkhard

Floris Books

Translated by Christian von Arnim

First published in German as
Das Leben in die Hand nehmen
by Verlag Freies Geistesleben, Stuttgart in 1992.
First published in English by Floris Books, Edinburgh in 1997
Fifth printing 2023

 Also available as an eBook

British Library CIP Data available
ISBN 978-086315-253-5

Contents

PART TWO:
AN APPROACH TO LIFESTORY WORK

Foreword

Lifestory work has assumed great contemporary relevance. Many books and writings have been published on this subject, and the courses and lectures on offer are over-subscribed. For such work is important not only for people who find themselves in crisis situations, or who need help in coming to terms with the burden of ill health. It also provides help for those who want to deepen their self-knowledge while stimulating and broadening their interest in and understanding of other people and the circumstances of their lives.

The author writes wholly on the basis of her practical work; her experience as a doctor is clearly evident throughout and provides the background to the book. She speaks directly on the basis of her own study of anthroposophy and its understanding of the human being, and the laws of biographical development set out there. Her purpose is to bring the illuminated moments in each lifestory, as well as the shadow sides, to consciousness in such a way that people are enabled to gain access to both sides of life and can thus integrate the bad and more sombre aspects by recognizing their value in their own lifestory. In doing so, she always bases her descriptions and examples on real-life situations and stimulates readers to continue reflecting on their own and to take hold of their own individual lifestories as working material. The second part of the book describes the methodology for working on one's own lifestory, enabling everyone to begin such work.

Gudrun Burkhard is the founder of anthroposophical medicine in Brazil; she is also the founder of the successful Clinica Tobias, which has become a centre of anthroposophical medical work there. In recent years she has devoted her efforts wholly to the care of cancer patients, to dietetics and to lifestory work. The Artemisia clinic for recuperative care and after-care was founded with this in mind. Since then she has extended her course work and lecturing beyond Brazil to Europe, where she is regularly invited to participate in lifestory work, particularly in Switzerland, Germany, Spain and Portugal.

Gudrun Burkhard has always endeavoured to place her medical work in Brazil into the spiritual context of the objectives of the Medical Section at the Goetheanum. May her perspective on lifestory work fit constructively into the range of publications on this subject.

Michaela Glöckler, 1992

Preface

This book is dedicated in gratitude to my teachers Rudolf
Steiner and Ita Wegman, Norbert Glas, Rudolf Treichler and
Bernard Lievegoed. And in particular to Helmut J. ten Siethoff
who fifteen years ago provided me and my husband with the
foundations for our lifestory work.

Above all, gratitude is due to the many people who
entrusted themselves to our work and whose rich lives made
this book possible. My thanks are also due to my first husband
and companion Peter Schmidt and our four children, as well as
to my second husband Daniel Burkhard, my companion in the
happy and difficult times which we faced together.

Thanks also to all the staff of Artemisia, the institution
established for our work in Brazil.

Lily Wilda and Suzana H. Lüchow also helped to bring the
book to print. The drawings are by Michael Seltz.

Gudrun Burkhard

Introduction

When two friends meet who have not seen one another for a long time, they mostly spend some time catching up with what has happened to each of them. They talk about the things they have done and their personal experiences up to the moment they met. You, dear reader, have no doubt done the same.

In this way things which have long been forgotten are recalled again. We ask questions and make comments on the subject under discussion. The conversation proceeds like two rivers which touch here and there, intermingle, interchange and then pursue their individual courses again. We could continue talking like that for hours. Why is such a conversation so refreshing? Our personality and that of our interlocutor are touched as if by magic, becoming alert and wholly present. Our past lights up in us in the present and it frequently happens that this leads us to take fresh decisions and set new objectives for the future.

If we examine this natural process, which everyone has experienced, more consciously and in greater detail, we can start to work on our lifestory. This book is intended as an encouragement to create time at regular intervals — a process which may be spread over a period of years — to work on our own lifestory in the quiet of our room, out in nature, with friends, or together with other people on a course. It depends wholly on the situation in which we happen to find ourselves whether we want to concentrate mainly on ourselves or whether we wish to allow ourselves to be enriched by the experiences of others.

There are many biographies of important people, but the lifestory which is most important to each person is his or her own one. It is undoubtedly true that of the more than one thousand lifestories which we have heard in conversation, each one is different and unique, and each one is extremely interesting.

There is little benefit today in being a genius or having extraordinary gifts. Our own genius may benefit others or provide the world with new achievements. But it is of little use if we behave outrageously in a social context, constantly clash with other people, cannot get along with them, and are unable to develop personally. Genius flows in from the past; but by working on ourselves, by our encounter with other people and our behaviour towards them, we stride from the present into the future in a constant process of transformation. 'He's a genius — but impossible socially.' The behaviour of a person who might be described thus can no longer be justified today. A less gifted person who has to struggle to develop his capacities in life and has to work on himself will reap greater benefit for the future than the person who comes with enormous gifts but does not develop in any way.

A participant once asked at the end of a lifestory course: 'How can I prevent myself from falling in love with my lifestory?' In this respect it is important to bear in mind that the more we work on our own lifestory and learn to understand it, the more we will understand others. It is the same 'organs', as it were, which develop our understanding. Moreover, we experience how much we owe to others when we look back over our lives. They have made us what we are today. And that will fill us with a feeling of gratitude. We can extend this thought indefinitely. How much do we owe to our angel and the beings who have created the human being? How many times were we in danger of death and were rescued at the last moment? Many situations are the making of the sublime guides of our destiny who are wiser than we are. And when we look back at these situations in particular, with special gratitude, we recognize that we could never have managed them on our own.

Growing numbers of people today suffer from loneliness. The present time has led to our separation from the spiritual world. Our ancestors still had a natural relationship with the religious sphere. We, as modern, scientific people, have lost

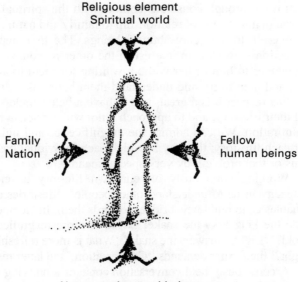

Figure 1.

this connection. At the same time we have left the old family bonds behind us. Everyone wants to go their own way today. It is increasingly rare for the younger generation to follow in the footsteps of the older one, that a son takes over his father's business. The feeling of national belonging is decreasing all the time. We are increasingly becoming world citizens in the widest sense of the word. Modern communications allow us to become aware in seconds of what is happening all over the world. We have also lost our natural contact to the earth, to nature and to its circumstances, which our ancestors still possessed. Indeed, we are destroying our natural environment.

Although we are constantly among people, we feel lonely and have little contact with them. We are faced with the big question: How can we overcome that loneliness? We can do that only through conscious contact with the spiritual sphere, through new forms of relationship to family and nature — and, above all, to our fellow human beings. The first step in this direction is to take an interest in the other person, to address ourselves to him or her without waiting for them to approach us, and then to try and understand them better as individuals. In this respect it is a great help to have a better understanding of their lifestory, and to approach it not with criticism but with admiration. We can admire the magnificence and uniqueness of each lifestory; the way in which each individual has solved this or that problem by very special means!

Working consciously on our own lifestory develops the capacity in us to understand other people's lifestories and that enables us to build new bridges towards them. In Goethe's fairy tale the king asks the snake: 'What is more magnificent than gold?' 'Light,' answers the snake. 'What is more refreshing than light?' the former demands. 'Conversation,' the latter responds.

A consciously held conversation contains a unifying element — it builds bridges.

The perspectives developed in this book are the result of many years of activity in which my staff and I have worked with many people in various groups. For fifteen years we have been offering courses in Brazil on lifestory work and on the laws which underlie biographical development. My lifestory at the end of the book sets out the path by which I came to do this work. The courses are inspired by therapeutic considerations. They are open to everyone, but are particularly intended for people who have encountered difficulties in their lives either of a psychological or physical nature. Many people who are in the middle of a professional or personal crisis also attend the courses. The individual lifestories reproduced in this book are authentic. They were drawn up by individual participants at the lifestory seminars.

The first part of the book sets out my observations on the way in which a person's life develops and gives an overview of the laws underlying biographical development. The second part of the book goes on to deal with the methodological structure of the courses and the way in which each individual can work on his or her own lifestory. The poems between the individual chapters may serve as leitmotifs for the work.

PART ONE

The Laws of
Human Development

Song of the spirits over the waters

The human soul
Is just like water:
It comes from heaven,
Returns to heaven,
And down to earth
It must again.
Forever changing.

Streaming from the high,
Steep rockface,
The pure flow
Bursts sweetly
In clouds of spray
On the smooth rock,
And, lightly caught,
It plunges downwards,
Creating veils,
With muted roar.

If cliffs tower up
Against its plunging fall,
It foams in anger,
Step-by-step
Into the depths.

In its flat bed
It meanders through valley
meadows,
And in the smooth lake
The stars
Feast their eyes.

Sweetly the wind
Woos the waters;
Mixing from depths
Foaming breakers.

The human soul,
How like the water!
Human fate,
How like the wind!

Johann Wolfgang von Goethe

1. An overview

Before we begin to work with lifestories in detail, it is helpful to acquire a general overview of the laws which govern the course of our lives as a whole. We will therefore begin with a broad outline of human biographical development.

A person's life can be divided into three main parts:
- The main characteristic of the first phase of human life is physical development. We, as individuals, are occupied at this stage above all with building our body and allowing our organs to mature physiologically. This period lasts approximately from conception to 21 years of age. We can also call it the 'receptive' or 'preparatory' phase. In this phase we do not contribute a great deal to our destiny. On the contrary, it is something which we bring with us from our past.
- Then we live through the middle phase in which we are primarily concerned with our soul development. In this phase we are faced with the major task of self-education and self-development. Our personality is no longer tied to the body in the same way. It 'comes of age' at 21 and is now able to determine and be responsible for the course of its life. This is when we live in a very 'expansive' phase, when we found a family, build a house, start work and build a career. This is also the phase when we have dealings with many people — that is, a phase in which we take our cues from social life. We learn from other people. We experience confrontation, love, enthusiasm, antipathy in our dealings with other people — feelings with which we have to learn to live and which we have to bring under the control of our ego. All these existential battles hone our soul to an ever greater degree: we achieve psychological maturity. This is the time during which we develop ourselves as individuals

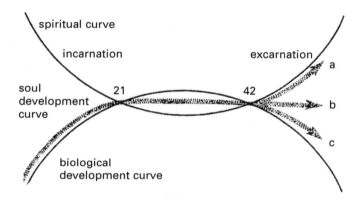

Figure 2.

in the world. We truly grow up only when we reach the end of
this phase. The generative and degenerative forces in our body
are balanced in this period of psychological development: that
is why we can be so productive in our external dealings.
– We then enter the third phase, the phase of spiritual development. Just as the plant spreads itself and bears blossoms and
fruit so the fruits of our life also have to become visible. We
have to allow them to become fully mature. During this period
the biological forces begin to weaken gradually and the degenerative forces in the body gain the upper hand. We not only
set out our own objectives in our soul and spiritual development, but we turn to greater goals. In other words, we set ourselves objectives in the wider context of human development.
Moreover, we begin to concern ourselves increasingly with
subsequent generations. Greater effort is needed to achieve
the goals we set ourselves in our development because in
this phase we are no longer supported by the life forces of
the body. But it is precisely this circumstance which allows

us to develop greater consciousness because the generative forces in the body act as a damper on the consciousness. We feel sleepy after a meal for example; or babies sleep almost the whole time and double their weight in the course of a year. But the more the body degenerates, the more consciousness we develop. Life forces are liberated all the time by the degenerative processes and they are available to us as forces of consciousness. (We have shown this development by line a in Figure 2.)

During this last stage of life the soul forces either accompany the growth of our consciousness or, if we do not work consciously on ourselves, they can become prey to the degenerative forces in the body. We can of course also ignore the degenerative forces in the body and continue to work with maximum effort. That can, however, lead to a massive breakdown after a few years (cancer, heart attack, stress, exhaustion, etc.) forcing us to take a rest. Thereafter we are forced to reorganize our lives. (Compare line b in Figure 2.)

In the animal world we can observe how creatures become useless and superfluous in this phase and wait for death. The fairy tale of the 'Town Musicians of Bremen' illustrates this process very well.

If as a human being I adopt the attitude: 'I'm already fifty-four — there is no point in starting anything new,' the development of my soul will begin to falter. (Compare developmental line c in Figure 2.)

But since human beings are not only biological beings, but also soul and spiritual ones, they have great developmental potential at this stage: 'Life begins at forty' is an apt saying to describe this state of affairs. The soul and spiritual forces are increasingly detached from the body during this period and we are increasingly free to develop new spiritual capabilities.

To avoid misunderstandings, of course there is also soul development in the first 21 years. But it is strongly associated with the body. Even the spiritual element of our personality begins to make an appearance. And of course our soul development continues in the phase of spiritual development, in the third phase, and much that we failed to do in previous years can be made up. Moreover, we cannot understand the phase when the soul develops if we do not take the 'I' into account which constantly works on the transformation of the soul. Body, soul and spirit ('I') thus always act together.

The three great phases in life can also be characterized as follows:
– Taking and receiving predominates in the first phase. It is a time of preparation, of 'human development.'
– The interaction between giving and taking comes to the fore to a greater extent in the second phase. It is the time of living and battling, of 'being human.'
– The emphasis is on giving in the third phase. It is the time of 'human fulfilment.'

These three phases have been known about since ancient times. They are described as spring, summer and autumn. A gardener who knows the seasons well also knows when this or that has to be sown and when the harvest can be brought in. Similarly, human beings who are aware of the phases of life will, like the good gardener, not want to harvest before the tree has grown properly and blossomed. In the spring all plants are still at the seedling stage and need much strength to grow. In the summer the plants spread out in nature, and in the autumn the fruits ripen and bear seeds. In winter the seeds rest in the earth and wait for new life.

If we divide human life into two halves, we can say that until the age of 35 everything is in preparation mode — it is like a great intake of breath. The body breathes in its spiritual individuality. We may describe this process as incarnation (see Figure 2).

From 35 onwards the mode changes to one of giving — we give back to life and the people who surround us those things which we have received and allow them to bear fruit in the world. The great process of breathing out begins. That development may be characterized as one of excarnation (compare

Figure 2). It is an interesting point that our lungs possess their greatest capacity at this point (at around 35), which then gradually begins to reduce. Sports people often reach the climax of their ability at this point.

The human lifestory can also be compared to a daily rhythm. We gradually wake up from sleep and begin to open ourselves to the world. We first have to warm up our body so that we are fully present in it and are fully in control of it, rather like a musician first has to warm up his instrument before he can produce beautiful tones from it, or a sports person first has to warm up before taking part in a competition. This is followed by the productive hours of the day which, rather like the productive years in life, fall into the middle phase. In the evening we gradually withdraw from our bodies, we become tired and sink into sleep — or, in terms of our life as a whole, into death.

In the middle of our life something takes place which might be called a change in direction of our values. Previously we assimilated knowledge from the outside; we subsequently return these values to our surroundings in transformed and purified form as wisdom.

It can often be experienced that small children are surrounded by something like an 'aura' which encounters the world in complete innocence and is enchanted. In some older people on the other hand we encounter a certain radiance and luminance — if they possess inner spiritual contentment and balance — which comes from the inside. That which was on the outside is grasped from the inside towards the end of life.

Human beings gradually come down to earth in the first half of their lives. Education and environmental factors should contribute to a strong and healthy body, one with solid ground under its feet. The healthy body then provides the basis on which human beings can develop a balanced soul and spiritual life. In the second half of life it is increasingly spiritual awareness which contributes to the harmony of a person's being, even if the body sometimes already suffers from illness and the disabilities of old age. In this phase of life, balanced soul and spiritual behaviour forms the basis for physical well-being.

These three major phases can, in turn, each be subdivided into three smaller ones, giving a period of seven years. We become aware of considerable changes in life after seven years and we have to learn to pay attention to them.

The division of life into seven-year phases figures in many past traditions. Rudolf Steiner took up this way of looking at things again and validated it on the basis of the science of the spirit. Special changes take place at the beginning and end of each seven-year-period which are mainly physical in the first major phase, but which become evident on a soul level in the second phase and on a soul and spiritual level in the third. We will look at this in greater detail in the chapter 'Rhythms and mirror images' (see page 139). We will take particular account of the seven year rhythms in the lifestory case studies. In order to avoid a purely theoretical approach, we will constantly observe lifestories and gradually develop the theoretical concepts.

We will now attempt to feel our way into the biographical element by means of a number of lifestories.

Lifestory 1

I was born in Portugal in a small village near Coimbra. It was very green there, with trees, and the mountains were not far away either. It was a lovely, peaceful place. I am the third child and have two brothers, one of whom is three years older and the other fourteen months.

My first memory: It was approximately at my second birthday when my little sister was born. I heard my mother's screams who was probably in labour. My older brothers were away and I felt very lonely. I climbed on to a chair to look out of the window. The view was of mountains and valleys. Suddenly I saw the Mother of God with a red dress and blue cloak. I was very frightened and ran away.

When I returned to that house at the age of 68 I saw exactly that window and chair and felt a slight shiver run down my spine. I can still see the picture before me exactly as it was then.

After three years another sister was born.

When I was three years old my father lost all his possessions. We moved to my grandparents' house in Aveiro. My father then went to live in Brazil, in Bahia. I was four years old at the time. Finally we — my mother, who was pregnant again, and my four brothers and sisters — followed my father to Salvador (Bahia). There my two younger sisters died within one week of each other from a bacterial diarrhoeal illness after we had drunk contaminated water. In the following week my mother gave birth to my new little sister. Since the little one was zealously taken care of to compensate for the loss of the other two children, I was, of course, very jealous.

When I was five years old, the whole family moved to Rio de Janeiro, but things were very difficult there. My mother was not very healthy either. So she decided to return to Portugal with the four children and all of us lived in the house of my grandparents in Aveiro once more. My father remained in Brazil and worked as a sales representative. Later he moved to São Paolo.

Aveiro is a very beautiful town with many flowers and it is very clean. The town is bisected by the branch of a river which presented a great attraction to us children because it was busy with many ships and boats which were decorated with designs. It was a particularly colourful life. My brothers went to nursery school in Aveiro and I attended primary school in a convent. After the first four years I was sent to another convent school where I learnt Portuguese well and hand work. Then, at age eleven, I became ill: I got paratyphoid fever.

In the meantime, my father had opened a ceramics factory in São Paolo and was manufacturing water filters. Later

*he bought the company 'Salus' which purified and sterilized
water. He produced filters, then, to sterilize water.*

*[It is interesting how a negative experience in this person's
destiny — the death of the two daughters through contaminated water — is turned into something positive here.]*

*My childhood was somewhat sad in Aveiro for my little sister
was the subject of all attention and I always felt somewhat put
in the shade. Today I understand that this child was like an
angel for my mother since she had lost the other two children.*

*After six years we returned to Brazil but this time we went
directly to São Paolo. I was almost twelve years old. As I
said, my father owned the filter factory. At twelve I menstru-
ated for the first time. I was also sent to another convent
school, São José, in order to repeat the fourth pre-school
year. I do not have happy memories of that time in school.
I was put in the shade again, felt myself as an outsider and
pushed aside. For when I returned from Portugal, I had a
very strong Portuguese accent. [Brazilians speak quite a different, much softer Portuguese.]*

*Thus I became an object of mockery for my fellow pupils. In
history lessons the nuns always complained about the Portuguese. I became very angry and upset by that and reproached
my father for having taken me away from Portugal. I even
made secret plans to return there. During this time I turned
inward very much and became very introverted.*

*At 14 I began a secretarial course in order to become a
secretary. My mother was working in a business during this
period. When I was 16, my mother started a sales office for the
water filters. This was 'Casa Salus' and I began to work for
my mother in the office during the afternoons. In the morning
I took English and piano lessons. At that time I was already
made responsible for looking after the cash and all the written
work, as well as for the business accounts. I was very happy
during this period, blossomed in my work and thought myself
very important. Financially, too, I was independent.*

When I was about 18, I undertook a long and beautiful trip to Portugal with my parents and brothers and sisters. It was a great pleasure for me to visit my relatives and the places of my childhood. When I returned, I continued to work, resumed my studies, received my money and was able to buy what I wanted, mostly imported things. I felt happy, independent and important. But in spite of all this I began to feel a great void in my life. That made me sad. Somehow I felt useless, superficial and empty. I wanted to help and have the feeling that someone needed me. Sometimes I travelled to Rio de Janeiro with my father, for we had an office there and my father had to visit the business. Family life continued in this fashion — my brothers married and nephews began to arrive.

It was not until I was 25 that I met the man whom I would later marry and who now gave meaning to my life. I was not madly in love but I had great sympathy and admiration for him. Slowly a deeper love, a solid and beautiful love began to develop. But I did not marry until I was 28. It was exactly on my marriage day that my father was absent and suffered a heart attack on his journey. He travelled to Portugal once more during this year and died in Aveiro in my grandparents' house when I was 29. That is also where he was buried.

My life continued in the same fashion between work and home.

I very much admired the intelligence of my husband, his way of working, his character, his morality. He was very kind, but also very jealous.

When I was 31½ I fell ill with a serious intestinal infection with a temperature of over 40 degrees. Once again I had the same dream as I did with my childhood illnesses, that is, measles and paratyphoid. I dreamt that I was climbing higher and higher until I reached heaven. There I was met by Peter, a very nice, older man with a beard and white hair, who opened the door of heaven for me. It was beautiful. Wonderful sounds, white flowers. St Anthony also came towards me and he was unforgettable and indescribably beautiful. Suddenly someone told me that I could not stay there yet, that I had to return. That is when I woke up and screamed. I kept falling, faster and faster, fell on barbed wire and became covered in blood. I felt fear and terror on each occasion when I woke up after that. Since childhood, since I was about six years old, I have always had the same dream with the same details. I became aware of this when I was 31½, after that serious intestinal infection. Thereafter I spent some time in my mother's house where I recuperated from the illness. In the same year, when I was 32, my husband fell ill with a kind of polyneuritis and had to undergo a spinal puncture. It took a long time until the exact diagnosis was arrived at. Three years later my husband — he had still not been properly diagnosed — began organizing spiritualist sessions and trying all kinds of things. He was suspected of suffering from infectious rheumatism but all the investigations brought no positive results. My husband was extremely aggressive, rebelled and wanted to commit suicide. During this time Dr Alexander Leroi came to Brazil on a lecture tour. He suspected that my husband had multiple sclerosis. His suspicion turned out to be correct. My husband suffered this illness for 15 years. This gave me the task I had wanted: being useful and being able to help someone.

In my thirty-sixth year we travelled to Switzerland. My husband stayed in the Ita Wegman Clinic in Arlesheim for nine months. We met important people there and also began to study anthroposophy. When I was 37, we spent some additional months in my grandparents' house in Aveiro. Thereafter we returned to Brazil. My husband had to use a wheelchair by that time. He continued with the anthroposophical treatment in São Paolo, including massage and curative eurythmy. Sometimes he felt better, sometimes worse. While I was looking after him I felt that I had changed very much. A wonderful spiritual love developed between us which is so strong that it will never end. In the morning I looked after my husband and in the afternoon I pursued my work. During the 15 years of his illness he was the instrument of my purification, my spiritual elevation, maturity and cleansing. Never again in life did I consider myself insignificant, empty or unhappy. I felt great inner harmony and the strong link with my husband reached beyond death; it has given me strength, protected and guided me to the present day.

When I was 43 my mother came to live with us. One year later my husband and I were together once more on a farm with my relatives. My husband was not well there and from that time onwards he no longer left his own house.

A year later, my nephew died tragically at 19 in a car crash. We were witnesses at the wedding of another nephew. A further nephew represented my husband at the altar. I was 47 years old when my mother began to suffer from heart trouble. Furthermore, my domestic, who had been with us for years and who had looked after my husband from childhood, suffered from highly ulcerous varicose veins and had to undergo surgery. Thus I took on the care of three people in the house. My husband's paralysis continued to progress. He finally died on 4 June 1970. I was just 48 at the time. We were together for 22 years. He was my best friend.

After the death of my husband I threw myself completely into my work and built up several branches of the company. In the end I had four large shops under my control which I administered. From the age of 56 onwards I began gradually to give up this work and finally only kept one business.

Addition (written at 85, in 1985):
I still manage this one shop. I have finally learnt to give others more autonomy. I love the contact with the customers. In the evening I go home where I live alone. I feel somewhat lazy and 'too established.' I do not want to feel useless and want to find a new task. I have not had a holiday for nine years. I would like to travel to Switzerland and Portugal once more.

But this holiday only happened after a further three years, and, thirty years after her visit to Switzerland, Mrs L returned to

Arlesheim. She visited the Clinic and the Goetheanum, and there spent most of her time studying the carved wooden statue of the 'Representative of Mankind' by Rudolf Steiner. On her return journey through Portugal she stayed once more in the house in which she was born. She decided to sell the last of her shops when she returned to Brazil. After all, she had worked twenty-eight years without a break, from 1960 to 1988. Her parents' business was given to a nephew.

Key lifestory information

2 years:	First memory (spiritual experience).
3 years:	Her father moves to Brazil.
4 years:	She goes to Brazil herself — loss of two sisters.
5 years:	Return to Portugal.
11 years:	Paratyphoid.
12 years:	Return to São Paolo, Brazil.
14 years:	Secretarial training.
16 years:	She begins to work.
18 years:	Journey to Portugal. Visit to places of her childhood.
25 years:	She meets her future husband.
28 years:	Marriage, death of father.
31½ years:	Intestinal infection — supersensory experience.
32 years:	Husband falls ill.
36 years:	New stage — becomes acquainted with anthroposophy in Arlesheim.
37 years:	Journey to Aveiro, Portugal.
43 years:	Her mother moves in with her.
48 years:	Death of husband — business built up.
56 years:	Gradually hands over business to others. Keeps one (no holidays).
63 years:	Intensive work in one business (no holidays).
66 years:	Journey to Goetheanum, Ita Wegman Clinic and Portugal — Decision to hand over last of businesses (to nephew).

This account might well be described as a lifestory without any great dramatic events. Why, then, did we choose to
include it here? Because we kept up with Mrs L over many
years and because she was able to work on her own lifestory
for a number of years. Some typical laws may be observed in
this lifestory.

Let us look at the laws of the first three seven-year-periods.
The environment in which Mrs L lives increasingly expands.
House, school, life (job) are three steps in which she continuously
develops as she grows up. She becomes shy and introverted at the
age of 12 due to the mockery of the other children and because
she feels 'different.' Mrs L begins to work at 16 and one can feel
that the motif which is present throughout her life — business —
starts here. Nevertheless, she feels unhappy and empty.

She marries at 28 and her father dies — the old is left
behind, there is a new start. The connection with her partner
in life presents her with new challenges after three-and-a-half
to four years: care of an invalid for 15 years which enables her
to come to a spiritual view of the world and to purify her being
in devotion and love.

It is only after the death of her husband that Mrs L takes up
the leitmotif of her life again, business. In the course of seven
years (from 49 to 56) she gradually expands her business into
four large sales centres, slowly withdrawing from work after
the age of 56. She continues to manage the one business which
she keeps for another seven years.

A further thing we notice in Mrs L's lifestory are the inci-
sions made by the lunar node. (Every eighteen years a lunar
node is repeated in the human lifestory, something to which
we will return in the chapter on *Rhythms and mirror images*.)
At these points a stronger urge develops in Mrs L to visit her
homeland, the house of her grandparents, the places of her
childhood. That happens both at 18 and at 37! At 57 the wish
recurs, but can only be realized at the age of 66.

A Saturn rhythm also becomes visible in Mrs L's life (a
break or recurrence after thirty years): after thirty years she

once again seeks out the site of her spiritual home, the Ita
Wegman Clinic and the Goetheanum.

Lifestory 2

*I was the seventh child among twelve brothers and sisters. My
father was an indigenous Brazilian, my mother Portuguese. I
lived with my indigenous grandmother in a little hut behind
the family house. We, grandma and granddaughter, went to
the woods every day to collect herbs and edible fruits and to
search above all for tobacco plants. I had to spin the threads
for my grandmother which she used for her spinning. When the
tobacco was ripe, the leaves were picked. I had to roll them up
and my grandmother made large black sausages from them.
The tobacco was used for healing purposes but also for my
grandmother's pipe. She was a healer; many indigenous people came to her to collect advice and herbs for their illnesses.
All patients were treated with a little verse. Thus I learnt all
about medicinal herbs at an early age as well as the verses for
every wound. My grandmother had made me into her successor
although I was not her favourite granddaughter. She loved one
of my light-skinned sisters above all and often took her on her
lap and cuddled her. But my sister was not allowed to enter
my grandmother's house; I was the selected one who was to
succeed the healer.*

*Every evening I looked through the cracks of the 'Oca' (the
traditional house) where the indigenous people came to do
their singing for the evening ritual. No one was allowed to be
present. The rest of the family had to hide in the house.*

*When I was six I taught myself to read and write and my
father taught me arithmetic and other skills.*

*When I was nine, my grandmother came back from the
woods one evening. She was tired and lay down in her ham-
mock, had her son called and said that she would now die.
She did not accept the last sacrament. After her death she was
laid out in the main house by the family. Once she had been*

*buried, something completely unexpected happened: my father
set her hut on fire. Everything was burnt and only some ashes
remained. What, then, happened to me?*

*From this time onwards my family grew poorer and poorer.
My father bought himself new clothes and went promenad-
ing in town with other women. I had to feed the whole family
because I knew about the roots and fruits of the forest.*

*My father also became involved in politics. The govern-
ment changed and my father came under threat. Now I had
to accompany him as his bodyguard. I hid his revolver in a
small bag which had been woven by my grandmother. When I
was eleven years old, my father gave me a small revolver with
a mother-of-pearl handle. I quickly began to practise target
shooting. Our family, which had in the meantime built up a
chicken breeding business, had to watch as I used one chicken
after another for target practice, with my mother getting angry
because she had to cook the chickens instead of selling them.
But basically I helped as much as I could and sold many chickens for the family. I was very willing to help and very keen to
acquire knowledge. I began to help the surrounding farmers
to learn to read and write. When I went to school I skipped the
first three classes and was always the best in my class. I made
no friends. I pleaded with my father to be allowed to go to sec-
ondary school. I had to sit a difficult exam and passed. I was
the first woman in the family who was allowed to study. In sec-
ondary school, too, I turned out to be the best pupil. I earned
the money for my keep by working in the school canteen and
gave private tuition to many children. I also continued to teach
the farmers to read and write.*

*One day, some older people noticed me and brought me
mysterious books. They were books by 'Big Brother.' I was surprised by all these ideas. Gradually I began to teach the farmers
these ideas. I spoke on the radio and founded a newspaper. In
this way I became increasingly known in the country until one
day the military government became aware of me. They would
have liked to get rid of me. I fled and hid. But my naive father*

gave away my hiding place. I had to stay in prison for one
year — from 17 to 18. Finally, I was released and travelled to
a foreign city. There, together with some clergy, I worked with
farmers, teaching them to read and write. The farmers found it
difficult to hold the pencil with their rough hands. I rubbed fat
into their fingers so that they became supple again. The farmers
finally learnt to write their names and they began to develop a
greater awareness of what was happening in the world.

'Big Brother's' ideas became too constraining for me.
A guerrilla movement was being planned and developed at
this time. A trail was built for it which stretched far into
Paraguay. Many farms lay along its route which offered
protection to the guerrillas. I was eagerly involved in
planning this until I was thrown into prison again at 19.
This time I served two years which were harder than the
first time. I imposed an oath of silence on myself. And I
succeeded in not saying anything about the people I had
worked with, although I was severely tortured. My skin
became blotchy and developed wounds which refused to
heal. I developed fevers and rheumatic illnesses despite
much medical treatment. I lost so much blood when I was
injured on my leg that I had to be taken to hospital. No illness was found although I was intensively examined. After
six months in hospital I managed to escape. I was just 21
years old. I fled through several South American countries
until at last I found my life partner in one of these countries.

I married and became happy. My husband brought a stepson
into the marriage. Soon I became pregnant and gave birth to a
beautiful child. I was radiant with happiness as a mother. But
two years previously I had been diagnosed as suffering from an
illness: lupus. It kept reappearing in the following years but did
not bother me too much. I continued to enjoy teaching.

I resumed my studies in a South American country and
passed my diploma in sociology. But my life became increasingly dangerous and it was no longer enough to hide in South
America. So I fled to Europe where I settled in three countries,

one after another. I continued to teach but also began to work in a publishing house. My life was quite satisfying but my longing for my homeland was growing.

One day I was shown a film in which I stood at the airport seeing the children off to Brazil. The film with its emotional content was intentionally shown to me. But I rebelled and refused to continue watching the film. I was in control again. During this time an exile law was adopted in Brazil which meant that exiles, including me, were allowed to return home. My family gave me a touching reception at home. I was just 28 years old.

Life in my home country was a new experience for me. New people, the attempt to understand the country. In addition, my husband was unable to find work. He required some time to adapt to the new situation. I began to teach and in this way earned the money needed by the family. After a time, my husband began to behave increasingly strangely. He was an exile and women found that fascinating. One day he brought home a high-heeled beauty. He even wanted to live with both of us. I no longer accepted that and moved out with the two children. I was deeply depressed and unhappy. I still loved my husband and was unable to understand how he could grab the first woman that came along and abandon his own wife after all we had been through.

I was about 30 when I separated from my husband. It took two years for me to regain my inner equilibrium. Then I began to enjoy my work again. I also started to work in the film business and in advertising. Furthermore, I made lovely Brazilian confectionery which a friend sold for me. Thus I was well able to earn a living for me and my children.

I was almost 35 years old when I fell violently in love again. But this love was not to be. I had become pregnant but lost the child at three months. During this time my husband took the two children. The greatest crisis of my life began. I was alone without my children and felt a growing inner emptiness, a longing for something different.

*I had abandoned politics completely. Slowly I felt a new
seed beginning to grow in my soul. I began to search for
the spiritual element once more which my grandmother had
planted in me — the spiritual truth of finding oneself. My
children returned to me and the house filled with life again.
Also, I became acquainted with my new partner during this
time — at approximately 38 years of age. We were two souls
and one heart and complemented one another completely.*

*Thus the little girl Tanga has turned into a mature woman
who is consciously taking hold of her life at age 39 and is
seeking new values, who understands the seriousness of her
sickness and is trying to overcome that sickness with the help
of these new, spiritual values.*

What can we see in this lifestory? We experience a child who
is treated like an adult, who is confronted with great responsibilities at an early age; who does not live with her family and
brothers and sisters, but apart from them with her grandmother
who needs her and wants to pass on to her the grandmother's
gifts and responsibilities.

At age nine Tanga experiences how her home is burned
after the death of her grandmother and a completely new life
begins. Now she is faced with even greater responsibilities.
She is exploited once again, this time by her father, and later
by politicians. She is always available to them. She faces difficult experiences in prison. To a certain extent she is protected
by her innocence here, but that does not prevent her from falling seriously ill.

Then the patient lives through a phase with many inner
disappointments. Finally she finds herself again at the age of
37 and discovers an inner spiritual thread.

We will come to understand individual features as they crop
up in this lifestory more exactly in the following chapters.

2. The developing human being: Up to the age of 21

The initial years of development to adulthood, that is up to about 21, exercise a formative influence on the whole of a person's life. A human being is born into a specific family, sees the light of day in a particular country and begins by learning the language of that country. Whether the child is a single one or has brothers and sisters will play a very important role in the child's later individual and social development. There are a number of inner and outer factors which shape the human being. People supply their own inner factors as it were, body build is once such factor for instance. However, these factors are also connected with what is inherited from the parents. Temperament, the influence of the zodiac and the planets are other factors with which a child is born. We will return to this below, on p.174.

The task of the individual in the first seven years is to transform his or her body. We can compare this process with the urge we might have to make changes in our home on returning from a journey which has made us change inwardly. Or another comparison: We ask an architect to build a house for us but shortly before it is finished we turn it inside out to make it as we want it. The individual faces a similar task. A person's self is of spiritual origin and comes to earth in order to transform the physical body, which is characterized by the paternal and maternal hereditary forces. We know from anthroposophy that this transformation process is helped along by the childhood illnesses which occur in the first years of life. In the first seven-year-period a renewal of substance takes place in which every cell in the body is given its individual character. Once we lose the more solid cells of our body, the milk teeth, in this process, it is a sign that the transformation is complete. The second set of teeth are quite individual in character and every dentist can recognize patients by the form of their teeth.

The spiritual awakening in the body which takes place in the first seven years is the result of external influences. We might draw another comparison at this point: How do we react when we jump into cold water? We receive a shock and contract into ourselves. But if we lie in a nice hot bath we are happy and stretch out in enjoyment. The same is true of the child's personality. If external sense impressions provide good and beneficial influences children will feel comfortable in their bodies and will extend themselves. If these sensory impressions are unpleasant and act like a cold bath, the individual withdraws from the body and there is insufficient transformation of the body. Often that only becomes clear in later years.

Human beings learn through imitation in the first seven years and the attitude of adults is very important. This is the time when the basis for moral behaviour in later life is formed.

Rudolf Steiner spoke about the importance of the first seven years in many lectures and courses. He illustrates very well how during this phase the child can experience that the world is good through the effect both of sensory impressions and the moral behaviour of adults!

What do children need for their spiritual development in the first seven years? A participant at one of my courses expressed it in the following way: They need a nest. And what do nests offer? They offer warmth, envelopment, protection, a regular pattern of eating and sleeping, and, above all, love. These are all conditions which the family or parents should create for the child in the first seven years because children are totally dependent on their external surroundings. It is quite wonderful to see how children will gradually extend their limits. At first they exist in the maternal body, then in the cot, then in the room. After a time they crawl down the stairs and conquer the house, then the garden, followed gradually by the street and, if it is a small place, the whole village in time. The initially small and protected world of the child has expanded. We might also describe it as a gradual progression towards freedom which will be repeated many times in life.

The three fundamental capacities in the child — walking upright, speaking, and thinking — develop through imitation; in the first three years of life, human beings are presented with their most outstanding qualities by the gods. It is only when we break a leg so that we can no longer walk, or become so hoarse that we lose our speech, or if our thinking or memory is impaired for some reason, that we notice how much we depend on those three qualities and what they mean to somebody who has been denied them by nature. All these things are given to us as a gift before our human consciousness is even capable of perception. We use them to conquer time, space and eternity. We might also say: We learn to move — in space, in our intercourse with other people and in our world of thoughts. 'I am the way, the truth and the life,' says Christ.

Directly after this first phase, at approximately three years of age, the first experience of self occurs. The sensory nervous system has matured and the human individual can use it as an instrument. The child separates itself inwardly from the world and experiences itself as an 'I'. It is no longer 'Katie wants,' but 'I want.' This is when the child enters the all too familiar difficult age. (If, even as adults, our response to everything is 'No,' this probably has something to do with the necessity of asserting our self.)

Human beings are capable of memory from the first experience of self onwards. The thing which is remembered first in a person's lifestory is generally decisive for the whole of their destiny. It is very important when we begin to work on our own lifestory that we try to recall our first memory. Indeed, methods are used today which try to delve into memories of our life before birth and previous incarnations. But that is not what we are after here. We are observing our ordinary waking consciousness. And here it is exceptional if people remember, for example, the time when they were carried as infants in their mothers' arms.

It is already obvious from the descriptions in the earlier life-stories that the environment, nature, and above all the parental home exercise a decisive influence on the child. Brothers and sisters already demand human interaction. Often there is jealousy and sharing has to be learnt. It becomes very clear in the first lifestory that the patient was the third child in a family. I recommend reading Karl König's book *Brothers and Sisters* in this respect. There König sets out the role which is typical for a third child. It always feels slightly at a disadvantage. This is also clearly evident in the third lifestory (p.74) and in Lifestory 5 (p.92).

What about the first memories in the lifestory descriptions? In Lifestory 1 the experience of the spiritual world is very pronounced. The experience of the Madonna exercises a decisive influence on the whole life of the patient. What a contrast to the childhood of the girl Tanga in Lifestory 2! Here there is no clear first memory.

What happens to the experience of trust in this first seven-year-period? After all, children are born with a very pure and natural trust. If they have climbed high into a tree and cannot get down any more, they call their parent or guardian and quite trustingly jump into their arms. When in life do we ever again have the trust to abandon ourselves to an adult in this way? Trust is part of the child's basic attitude. It is innate in a sense. How quickly, however, do we lose that trust! Perhaps the child wakes up in the middle of the night and their parent or guardian have gone to the cinema. Or the baby-sitter who is supposed to look after the child frightens her charge by saying: 'If you do not go to sleep, the black sheep will come and bite you.' Another example: Little Johnny has put his coat on to go to the circus and before he knows it he is sitting in the dentist's chair. Or another tale told by a participant at my course: He did not like to have his hair cut as a child. So every time that he went to the hairdresser the latter told him a long story about an aeroplane that he was building for the little boy. Once the plane was finished, both of them would go and fly in it. This went on for several years until someone told the boy one day: 'Listen, this plane doesn't exist.' This represented such a disappointment to the boy that he was unable to forget the incident for the rest of his life. In a certain sense it was this experience which brought the concept of mistrust into his life. It took him a long time to get over it.

Once the body has been worked on in the first seven-year-period, life forces are liberated which were previously needed to work on the body. Children are ready for school and receptive. They can now use these forces to acquire knowledge. There are seriously detrimental consequences if children go to school too early. These do not make themselves felt in the subsequent seven-year-periods but mostly later in life, in the phase between the ages of 56 and 63, for that is when these forces detach themselves from the sensory nervous system again. Overall we may say that the first seven years are decisive for later physical health in a person's life.

The respiratory organs mature in the second seven-year-period. These organs are the vehicle of our feelings which allow us to distinguish between sympathy and antipathy, between good and evil, beautiful and ugly. It is also the phase which is mirrored later in life in our relations with our fellow human beings and which reflects, above all, our relationship to the world. We might say that we learn to breath in and out during this phase. That refers not only to the respiratory process as such but to our relationship with the world as a whole. We no longer feel embedded in nature and at one with it; instead, a rich inner life now unfolds and we develop an increasingly fuller imagination. We experience the dramatization, as it were, of life in our childhood imagination — we are the princess, then the slave, then again the hero or the robber. Our soul begins to shimmer in many colours and our inner world is in constant interchange with the external world.

In this phase of life the children no longer learn wholly by imitation. But they need adults to look up to and experience as figures of authority. That may still be done partly by the parents, but the teachers in school also begin to fulfil such a role. School is the place where children spend a central part of their time between the ages of seven and 14. Teachers play an important role in their lives. Teachers become the mediators between the world and the child. What they tell the child or the view of the world which they transmit have a deep-seated effect on the child's development and level of education in later life. Whether a teacher is convinced that human beings have descended from the apes or whether he perceives them as divine beings with body, soul and spirit produces a radical difference in young people's perception of the world in the second seven-year-period. Whether a plant only consists of pistils and blossoms, etc., or whether the miracle of a flower produced by nature also exists to bring us human beings pleasure — all of these things have a decisive effect on later attitudes towards life in general. The world of the child's feelings must be included in the education process, in the lessons. A comprehensive literature exists on Waldorf education from this perspective which cannot, however, be dealt with in detail here.

If human beings experience a strongly authoritarian education at home and in school they have to 'breathe in' constantly, to continue with the image, and have great difficulty in 'breathing out'. This creates the risk that they become introverted. Later they have to work hard on themselves to come out of themselves again. If, on the other hand, education is too much lacking in authority, they are constantly 'breathing out' as it were. They develop too little inwardness in later life, become insufficiently reflective and are completely taken over by the external world. Thus the right degree, a rhythm between breathing in and breathing out, must be found. The best way to do this is if love is combined with authority in education.

Rhythm has always conferred vitality; it produces a healthy effect. But today many adults suffer from not having a proper daily, weekly, monthly or yearly rhythm. People complain about constant tiredness. Rhythmical disorders occur with increasing frequency — disorders of the sleep and digestive rhythm, cardiac-rhythmic disorders, asthma and so on. They probably originate in the second seven-year-period.

Art and religion play an extra special role in developing our feelings. The element of beauty must be brought to life in people during this period; thus Rudolf Steiner sums it up in his lectures on education.

The second seven-year-period is also the time when we are very much influenced by the behaviour of our fellow human beings, when all kinds of rules of behaviour become standards for our own life. Expressions such as 'You've got two left hands,' 'You are the black sheep of the family,' or 'There is no point in sending you to school, you just don't learn anything, you're stupid,' affect us deeply in our soul. We also absorb the habits which we experience in the people who educate us. This is the seven-year-period when our own habits are formed: whether or not we brush our teeth after a meal, eat much salad, and so on. And how difficult it is in later life to shed bad habits or detach oneself from deeply ingrained standards!

Let us look at some such standards. For example: 'You mustn't cry — you must be strong.' What effect does this have on the feelings of an adult man if this rule was imposed on him as a growing boy?

Or: 'You must not play with boys.' Or 'You may not study, only boys are allowed to study.' How is a woman to cope later in life or in a job, or how is she to ensure sufficient income for her family if such ideas were inculcated in her childhood?

A great change takes place at about the age of nine. We begin to withdraw into ourselves to a greater extent. I suddenly realize that I have different feelings from my sister, or I begin to become emotionally aware of my neighbour's family; I might suddenly notice that I am born into a poor family and that the

other one is richer; I might notice that my friend's parents
are much nicer to her than mine are to me; or I notice that
my brother hates the cat of which I am very fond — many
more examples could be quoted. We might describe it as our
individual feeling life beginning to awaken at this stage. We
go through a second ego-experience. It is important that our
feeling life should find fertile ground on which to grow. Such
fertile soil can be provided by art or religion, but above all
by loving authority which comes from parents and teachers.
Teachers are very important for our education. It happens
frequently that in later life we are left with a love for those
subjects which were taught by loved or respected teachers.

This second seven-year-period is also the time when the
difference between 'I' and 'you' has to be come to terms with.
This occurs mainly in the context of our fellow pupils. It is a
phase which is decisive for our psychological development
and maturity, particularly in relation to the period between 21
and 42, and for relations with other people in general. It is,
after all, our relations with other people which enable us to
grow in our soul life.

In Lifestory 1 we can see that a fundamental break took place
in the life of the girl during the second seven-year-period, at
the age of 11: the move from Portugal to Brazil and the inabil-
ity — mainly because of her foreign accent — to fit into the
new school environment. The rejection by her fellow pupils
made her very introverted. We can see here that the girl could
not cope with the demands made on her from outside.

The girl Tanga in Lifestory 2 grows up in quite different
circumstances. She too experiences great change at the age of
nine which is connected with the death of her grandmother.
The whole of her past is as if extinguished after this event and
completely new values govern her life.

We now come to the age of 14. Pre-puberty starts as early as
11 or 12 and then intensifies until 14. Young people undergo

considerable physical growth at this age. The start of puberty is different with each person. Entry to this stage of life is considerably more difficult to manage than at around the age of seven. At the transition from the first to the second seven-year-period there are some children who do not want to go to school. But this reluctance can be overcome by a good teacher. A deeper caesura occurs, however, when the age of fourteen approaches. It is as if we tumble to earth out of paradise. We might almost compare it to the Fall. Now clear differences also begin to emerge between male and female attitudes of soul. We might say that men are connected more strongly to the earth while women remain on a more cosmic level. These differences then continue to characterize men and women in subsequent years. In some lifestories, this period coincides with the first attempt to commit suicide. We might describe it as the young person encountering a threshold experience: either I find the way to earth and become active here or I recoil from this world and return to the spiritual world. It often happens that such a young person, let us say a young girl of twelve, will use a great variety of means — in the past it might have been playing with dolls, today, at worst, it is drugs — to avoid contact with the earth and to remain in this childhood, imaginary, illusionary, not-yet-adult world.

The organs which now develop are those of the lower abdomen, the genitals in particular, and above all the muscular and limb systems. The whole of the human being's muscle system is consolidated in this period. These are the organs with which we change the world, as it were. We use the digestive organs to process the substances from the physical world and form our own human substance. Here, too, we are dealing with muscle activity. We change the external world with our limbs and in a sense create a new world. They are creative organs. We are able to help a new human being to start life on earth with our sexual organs.

Young people are now torn between two opposing forces. On the one hand the ideal image of the human being arises very strongly in them. At no other time is it so strong as during adolescence. On the other hand strong forces manifest themselves in the biological sphere through the awakening of the sex drive. These two forces work in opposite directions in young people — they are pulled from one extreme to the other — and it is as if their souls were balanced in the middle. They become dissatisfied with the world and life; this comes to expression in rebellious actions. During this period young people are often very much introverted and seek answers to the questions: 'Who am I?' 'What am I doing on earth?' They no longer feel understood by their parents and they are no longer satisfied with their teachers. They think that they can find the answers to their questions in the external world and cultivate all kinds of 'isms' from Marxism to Buddhism.

When people feel isolated they seek the company of others, but this search for company in young people manifests itself in profound criticism of their environment. It is as if they sit locked up within themselves and shoot their barbs at the outside world no matter whom or what they hit. There is great inner force and they want to change the world and their environment, perhaps by introducing new habits into family life or perhaps by changing the world. It often happens during this period that the three soul qualities of thinking, feeling and willing diverge completely. Some young people lose themselves in thinking, pondering and philosophizing. Others devote themselves entirely to their feelings and beliefs — the various hippy movements are an example of that. Some young people become aggressive and destructive and cannot keep their will under control, frequently ending up by terrorizing their environment. That wild horse, their own will, can hardly be restrained. The search for truth begins. Parents and teachers can only stand up to this if they remain genuine. Every family relationship which is not quite right is noticed and there is no sense in trying to pretend that something is the case which does not accord with the real situation. Neither do young people any longer accept book-learning; they want real experience. They want to find truth in themselves, in their parents, in the world.

This seven-year-period is the time when we lay the foundation for our spiritual development in later life. From the age of fourteen onwards we take on increasing responsibility for our destiny. Every human encounter has a deep meaning in terms of destiny and must be respected and looked after. Everything which we do has its consequences. There is not much sense at this stage in forcing children to learn. If they have not learnt by themselves by this time, they have to bear the consequences. The principle of freedom must reign in education. But the steps to freedom are slow ones. We can speak of external freedom which young people gradually acquire for themselves. And to the extent that they can begin to assume responsibility they enjoy it too. We might say that freedom and responsibility are the two elements which are put on the scales — they have to be balanced. At the same time the most important element for understanding between two people, dialogue, must be intensively cultivated. We might argue, but should not forbid. Young people have to learn to act at their own discretion.

We can also speak of inner freedom which is particularly important at this age. The more free people feel at home and in the family, the less likely they are to have the need for external freedom. (The same is true, incidentally, for the relationship within marriage.) How often do we experience the following or similar scenes: a young person has his own room and might already be going to university. Suddenly he is caught unawares when his sister, who has just been divorced, returns to her parents' home with three children. Now he has to clear out of his room for his sister. Why him in particular? It is different if he offers to do so of his own free will after having discussed the matter with his parents. But if he is forced to do so it represents an infringement of his personal freedom which is no longer permissible at this age. Other examples: A young girl receives letters which she is not given directly but which are opened beforehand. Or her parents find her diary which was left lying on the table by mistake — this is, after all, the time when young people feel the need to entrust themselves to their diary — and notice on reading it that the fifteen- or sixteen-year-old girl is already having sex with her friends. The diary is burnt and the girl may be severely punished by her parents.

The relationship of trust must not be disturbed during this period. Sometimes parents succeed in turning into their children's friends, which in turn creates the basis for dialogue and trust. In other cases young people mostly find an older friend for themselves or a relative, in other words, someone with whom they can have a real talk as one adult to another. It belongs to the sphere of inner freedom that the other person is respected as an individual. How, indeed, can we ever grow up if we are forever treated as children! This is the time when we want to go out into the world, the time when many young people begin to travel and seek experiences of all kinds. They want to try and experience everything. Many forbidden things are done in secret simply out of the need to prove oneself, to find oneself. The question 'Who am I?' applies to all areas: religion, sex, work. It is difficult to decide which impulses come from one's parents and which ones come from oneself. Often young people need to leave home in order to see that more clearly and discover themselves.

We now come to the age of 19. At 18 years and seven months we pass through the so-called lunar node in our lifestory. The same constellation of sun and moon as at our birth is repeated. This enables us during this period to have a clear experience of our path of destiny. (We will return to that later. Compare p.147) During this time it seems as if the heavens open a little bit wider and we are able to recognize inwardly which occupation we want to follow on earth. We might also say that this represents the third birth of the 'I' in the sphere of the will and activity. How many times does it happen, though, that the complete opposite takes place! In some places restrictions are still placed on women and they are unable to develop their vocational potential, as Lifestory 2 shows. A father believes he has the right to decide his daughter's future and tells her what occupation she is to pursue. Some young people manage to rebel during this phase but others shut themselves off. Many fathers still expect the young person to take over the family business. But the question of what occupation to pursue is increasingly one which today each person can only answer for him or herself; it is not easy to find one's vocation. Sometimes parents must wait patiently for years before young people find their vocation. In some cases they may start studying various subjects only to abandon them again, until they finally find the right way and with it themselves. Otherwise they will never come to rest vocationally in later life.

This is the phase when the foundations are laid for the spiritual development of later years: self-education, search for ideal values and for values as such. The search for truth and authenticity is a great one. It has three aspects. First there is scientific truth. This is extremely important for our development during this period. It is accompanied by psychological truth which is increasingly arousing the interest of young people today. And finally there are the spiritual truths. They, too, are finding ever greater interest among young people. We may say that we have acquired the fundamental conditions for harmonious development and self-education in later years only if we, as young people, have had sufficient and balanced access to scientific, psychological and spiritual truth. This applies both to our soul development in mid-life as well as our spiritual development in our advanced years.

In Lifestory 1, Mrs L's nineteenth year is the time when she travels back to Portugal to inspect the past, as it were. She is 18 years old, exactly the time of the lunar node. The moon is in exactly the same position in relation to the zodiac and the sun's path as at her birth. At this moment Mrs L is able to grasp her spiritual task on earth. It is as if she sheds her past in order to be active in the world of her own volition. In this lifestory the visit to Portugal and thus the shedding of the past is repeated at 37, that is, while passing through the second lunar node.

And from age 56, from the third lunar node, Mrs L begins to withdraw gradually from active life and gives up her business activities one after another.

In Lifestory 2, Tanga has managed to get her way and she succeeds in becoming the first girl in the family to study — powerfully she breaks new ground for herself! But then she becomes involved in politics and is excluded from society for three years and forcibly 'incarcerated.' This is likely to be the main reason for her illness.

Under ideal circumstances, the first seven-year-period leads us to the experience: 'The world is good.' This is decisive for our deeper feeling of morality in life. The second seven-year-period gives us the basis for aesthetic feelings in life if it gives us the experience: 'The world is beautiful.' And if, in the best case, the third seven-year-period gives us the feeling: 'The world is true,' we are educated to display a sense of truth and to adopt a healthily critical attitude in life. These foundations provide human beings with the principles of goodness, beauty and truth which belong to humankind.

We might also think about what inhuman qualities are brought to the fore if the opposite poles are experienced in childhood: malice, ugliness and untruth. But in every lifestory light may be introduced into such a period and it can be integrated into the personality. Then we will discover that we did not experience only bad things in a given seven-year-period. Such a view is strongly emphasized by psychoanalysis. The 'illuminated times' should be sought with much greater emphasis. Colours arise only once the soul has learnt to experience itself in light and shadow. Many suppressed emotions and memories are recalled and may be integrated into our personality in this way. This gives us the opportunity to stop reacting at 40 as we did at ten.

We will give another example below which provides a good insight into this and the next phase of life. A young man of 26 tells his 18-year-old brother:

I have always been lucky in life, but now it seems to me that

I will have to make an effort if this luck is to be preserved. You have always suffered in life; it is time that you made a conscious effort to stop the things which make you suffer.

These words truly express the way in which things are presented to us on a plate until we are 21, or at least 18. In some lifestories things may be slightly more difficult, in others easier, which is then experienced as good luck. But if there appear to be many difficulties this is experienced as bad luck. After the age of 21, however, the transformation process begins. We begin to develop a feeling of responsibility in relation to the gifts and abilities which we have been given and start to transform them consciously. The 26-year-old has begun to feel a certain weight in his life and has become aware that he needs to make an effort to take his life a stage further. He makes the 18-year-old aware of the possibility of consciously transforming his destiny and turning it into something positive.

The process can start with quite simple things. If we prepare well for the challenges, we have a much better chance of meeting them successfully than if we make no effort at all. From 14 onwards all kinds of desires and wishes develop within us and emotions rise powerfully from below, from the metabolism. A confrontation arises between the ideal image of the human being which we have quite clearly before us in these years and the rising sexual drives and wishes which surface from the metabolism. The struggle tears us apart. Then, however, self-education begins.

I recall the situation of a 16-year-old boy who told me: 'Well, I could smoke and I am tempted to try smoking. But if I think of the strength needed to stop smoking again, I don't even want to start.'

Many people between 21 and 28 continue to suffer the consequences of the follies they inflicted on themselves in the preceding seven-year-period. These consequences now have to be consciously transformed. That applies to a person's occupation as well. Most people start to work in the period from 14 to 21. Their job matures in the period from 21 to 28 — through conscious work.

The ancient Greeks pursued the sport of charioteering. They regularly practised bringing the wild horses harnessed to the chariot under control. They did this to strengthen their 'I' so that it could tame the inner wild horses as well. Today many young people pursue water sports of one kind or another, sailing or surfing, in which they have to fight mightily against the wind or high waves to keep upright. Sometimes they do so in wild conditions and it is this, precisely, which challenges their forces of self and will. They test themselves: how long can I stay upright in these fantastic, foaming waves? Even today, we want to learn to control something outside ourselves at a certain age, just like the Greeks. Later we learn to master it from the inside. Another example: A musical instrument, too, has to be mastered if harmonious tones are to be produced. But in puberty all kinds of dissonances have to be experimented with first. There are also, of course, many people who remain stuck in this phase of their development.

We will encounter the consequences of such development in the next chapter.

The twenty-first year

I am not I.
I am the one
who walks at my side but of whom I do not catch sight,
whom I often visit
and then often forget.
The one who is calmly silent when I speak,
who is gentle in forgiveness when I hate,
who roams around in the place where I am not,
who remains upright when I die.

Juan Ramón Jiménez

The age of 21 is experienced in many different ways today.
Many people go through deep crises during this time. They
could be described as crises of finding one's self. The big
question which already crops up in the preceding seven-year-
period is: Who am I?

Many doubts and conflict situations arise: 'Am I the result
of my parents?' 'Did I choose this job because I wanted it or
because of my parents? My father wanted to be an engineer
but didn't manage it, and now I'm supposed to study engineering. Is that my wish or is it my father's wish within me?'
'Actually I am sick of all this stuff with the Church. I do not
want to adopt the religion of my parents — in fact, I don't
believe in God at all just now.' 'For years I had to attend a
Waldorf school, my parents are anthroposophists; but I'm not
interested in that. I want go my own way.' 'I'm tired of all this
business with angels and guardian angels.'

These are all statements which can assist a person in finding
him or herself. Many people leave their parents' home at this
stage which makes it easier for them to find themselves. Some
do not manage it and stay at home. Here, too, there are vari-

ous opportunities for people to find their 'I'. A person might work during the day and study at night or vice versa and not be at home for most of the time. His parents complain that he is using their house like a hotel. These parents should be told: 'Thank God for that, because this is one way for people to find themselves.' Other young people have mothers who want everything to be nice and tidy. That leads them — unconsciously — to try and demonstrate that this a stupid attitude: 'I will become the great messpot in the house and leave everything lying about on purpose. Mum will have to accept that she should stop being so pedantic.' Another person might lock himself in his room for a whole year, not talk to anyone in the family, and might occasionally consent to having a meal brought in. To ignore him hurts his feelings but neither does he want to be enveloped in love: 'Please leave me alone!' Serious psychological damage can also occur during this time, of course. We cannot go into that, however, since it would go beyond the scope of this book.

Instead, let us look at some statements from people who experienced this stage of finding themselves in a positive way:

When I was 21 years old, I felt that I should celebrate my coming of age in some way. I asked my parents for permission to go travelling and set out, as a girl all on my own, for the first time. Forty years ago such an attitude was something quite unusual in a South American country.

Another statement:

When my youngest son was 20, I asked him what changes he felt within himself. He said: 'I feel as if a light is beginning to shine in me. Those things which are dark in me are gradually beginning to shine.'

And another statement from the same boy:

I wonder where conscience sits? It seems to me as if it sits behind my head, that a voice comes from there which is my conscience.

3. Being human: Soul development from 21 to 42

At this age, many young people take their rucksack and go off on their travels. We can use this as an image of what happens on a soul level. We have a rucksack, ready packed, which was stuffed full in childhood. Now we have to carry it. But when we go off like this it is very useful to stop and look at what the rucksack contains: we find a pile of stones. All of us will probably have seen an amethyst or agate or another geode. From the outside they are grey and rough but when you look inside a wonderful crystals are revealed. The light falls inside and is reflected in all directions. If we take a single one of these crystals and polish it, the flood of reflected light becomes even greater. Does soul development not also mean for us that we take our rough stones, open them and start to polish them so that our souls increasingly become the mirror for spiritual light? All our encounters from 21 to 42 and beyond give us the opportunity to find ourselves through others, to polish our rough edges through others. One of the developmental tasks in the phase of soul development which, as we explained above, lasts from 21 to 42 is to wake up in our soul and polish it.

What else do we find in our rucksack? Tools for working which we have collected in school, at university and at home. We will come to realize that many of those tools will never be used. The best thing is to put them aside so that they do not add unnecessary weight to our rucksack. Other tools need to be sharpened, or polished. And we will also notice that some tools are missing. We must ensure that we have all the tools we need. That is a major endeavour which we undertake mainly in the phase from 21 to 28. But of course our tools need to be renewed, sharpened and polished throughout life.

What else is in the rucksack? In most cases our parents have given us food to take along. But it only lasts for a certain amount of time. It belongs to the development of psychological maturity that both men and women are able to keep themselves supplied in the long run. The best education which parents can give their children is to ensure that they become self-sufficient as adults. We might describe that as an education for effective living. In that case it no longer matters that our snacks run out after a while, and we will be capable of replenishing them whenever necessary.

What else do we find in the rucksack? Sometimes we put our hands in and something treacly, clay-like sticks to our hands. We quickly withdraw our hands — but should we not have the courage to look into the rucksack? What is it that sticks to us like that? Of course — it is the substance from the past which now needs to be washed off. It is the old prescriptions which we were given in childhood; they affected us particularly strongly in the second seven-year-period. As we have already seen, we hear some phrases more often than our name: 'There is no point in going to university, you're not clever enough.' 'You've got two left hands.' 'Boys should not cry.' Sometimes it can take a long time to convince myself that I am not too stupid to study. It is a label which my parents have stuck on me and which actually bears no relation to what I am. Nevertheless, it has to be washed off. Or I notice that I am actually quite clever with my hands. I always wanted to be a joiner, but you cannot of course be a joiner with two left hands. But now I notice that I am good in joinery; my hands are not half as clumsy as my parents tried to make out. Or I have been married for a long time and have a loving wife and children. Sometimes my wife complains that I lack feelings. Is that such a surprise when I was not allowed to cry, show feelings as a child? Now I have to work to bring them to the surface again.

Grimm's fairy-tale of 'The Frog Prince' or 'Iron Henry' can help us to gain an insight into how soul development should be understood in this phase. If we cannot free ourselves from the prescriptions which were placed on us in the second seven-year-period our soul remains caught in its own bands and cannot develop further. In the fairy tale of the 'Frog Prince' the princess has to break the rules imposed by her father. She throws the frog against the wall so that the true form of the prince can be revealed. On the way home the prince calls three times: 'Henry, the carriage is breaking,' but it is not the carriage, it is the iron bands which were placed around the heart of the servant when the prince was turned into a frog. We can only continue our development as individuals if we free ourselves from the norms and phrases which were imposed on us in childhood, which inhibit us and tie us into a straight-jacket. That is a difficult task of self-education which is part of our soul development, mainly in the phase from 28 to 35.

I put my hand into my rucksack again. I notice that something sticks like tar. The tar cannot be scrubbed off. What things are those? Well, I happen to be six feet or five feet and eight inches tall. There is no point in struggling against that. I should stop being bothered by things like that and accept them in future. Or my parents have given me a complicated name. There is no point in rebelling against that either. I have a melancholic or choleric temperament. I can work on my temperament, but it is part of me like my bent nose. My task is not to get all upset about that and fight against it; these things are simply part of who I am. I should take these elements positively and integrate them into my personality. To put it a different way, the choice of this or that set of parents was mine. There is little sense in rebelling against the mistakes of the parents at 40. For each obstacle in life also strengthens me if I learn to surmount it.

There are many other things to be discovered hidden in the rucksack. I leave it to each individual reader to find out for him or herself what they are. The following letter from a 21-year-old gives an even clearer impression of what we have just described.

Letter from a 21-year-old medical student

*I feel great changes in myself, both in the routines of my life
and in my inner and outer appearance. I was one of the best
pupils in class, got the best marks, until I suddenly became
aware that what I was learning at the time and the way in
which I was learning it, the things which the teachers were
doing and on which they placed great emphasis, were leading
me nowhere. At least nowhere in relation to studying medicine, which was my real aim. I felt how technology was taking
over and my head could no longer cope with so many concepts. I felt myself losing my sensitivity. I therefore embarked
on a new method. I no longer simply copied what the profes-
sors were saying, paid more attention and tried to extract the
key elements from the lectures, in other words, I tried to stop
simply being a copying machine. We have classes all day and
many subjects which are not particularly useful. I therefore
started to attend these classes less assiduously. People thought
that I was doing the wrong thing but I felt much better for it
and was able to use my time more constructively doing other
things which I found more interesting. The only thing is that
my marks have gone down, but I still feel that I benefit suf-
ficiently from the classes.*

*Another thing which bothers people is my appearance. I
found myself looking like a real doctor, found my face looking the same as those of my fellow students since they started
studying medicine like myself. They placed great emphasis on
their appearance. All had the same hairstyle and combed it in
the same way, they had moustaches, glasses and used special-
ist terminology when they spoke. I therefore decided to let my
hair and beard grow and take off my glasses. I sent my better
clothes home. People began to call me a hippie and I felt very
happy. I carry a simple bag which I like very much instead
of a briefcase with the badge of the university emblazoned
on it like everyone else. I try to develop many other qualities.
Something like an explosion occurred in me: the impulse to*

turn everything on its head. I have started to learn to play the guitar, have joined a drama group and am gradually developing a greater understanding of nature. I observe nature, the fields and the river whenever possible. I have also started to cultivate a small garden. I wanted to change everything. I have started to study homeopathy and have already done an acupuncture course and a parapsychology course. Before, I never left the house; now I have a group of friends of whom I am very fond. We talk at length. I lead a Bohemian life, go to bed late, have discussions and am getting to know many people. I am working in a homeopathic out-patient department. I have been feeling good for the last few months. I feel that everything has become much more human. I feel very enthusiastic, mainly in developing the abilities I learn from various people. I read anthroposophy regularly. I have already read Occult Science, The Education of the Child from the Standpoint of Spiritual Science, The Four Temperaments, The First Three Years of the Child *and other books like* The Body as Instrument of the Soul. *All of these things give me great inner wealth. I am also in a phase in which I am very interested in discovering my inner self and in educating myself. I have started psychotherapy and I am feeling very well. I try not to hide anything from myself and to open all my doors, to be extremely honest and to be as useful as I can in practical life. I also want to tell you that I am thinking of experimenting with drugs. I want to study psychiatry and I should get to know these things; but I am not sure about it yet. I have tried to understand why I want to do it, whether it is not a form of escape, but I do not think so. A few days ago, when I was a bit drunk with some friends, I observed something incredible: Namely, everything which I wanted to say and do I would have wanted to say and do even if I had not been drunk. A few years ago that would not have been possible. I am in an extrovert phase, dance even without drinking, which I could not do before. I am very lucky in some respects; before I was very melancholic and frequently thought about death. Today, in this explosive phase in which*

*I am now, I no longer think about death or only rarely. I am
still melancholic by temperament but I feel very good inside
myself. I think that I now have a greater love for things and
people. I like to talk with people and try to say what I feel and
think clearly and without ambiguity. I did not do that before.
I kept it to myself if people depressed me. Perhaps I am going
too far with myself, but this is how I really see things and what
I think about them, and perhaps this might be of some value to
your research about lifestory.*

The developmental phase from 21 to 28

We can call the years from 21 to 28 the phase of our journey-
man years. Many people go out into the world to broaden
their experience. In a certain sense we also journey back to
childhood once more and transform the experiences of the first
21 years in a reverse process. Thus the phase from 21 to 28
reflects the one from 14 to 21. Such a reflection can be found
in many lifestories. (Compare also Chapter 6: Rhythms and
mirror Images of life development, p.139.) The phase from
14 to 21 is a difficult one, as can be seen from the letter by
the medical student, a phase when we are weighed down and
life often seems difficult. Young people feel that those around
them do not understand them and feel isolated. Often they also
feel depressed. At 21 young people enter another phase of life.
It is the time in which they tend to become extrovert and want
to try out all kinds of experiences and learn from life itself.

There are parallels to the first seven-year-period in certain
aspects of soul. When we learn to walk we fall over, stand
up again, fall over again and so on. In the fourth seven-year-
period we do the same on a soul level; we gain experience, fall
over, stand up again, gain further experience. Young people are
still insecure in their experience and must learn from it. They
are keen to live and want to experiment in a variety of fields, be
it work, relationships or even drugs and spiritual experiences.

We take greater control of educating ourselves. It is like riding a wild horse. We succeed only gradually in reining it in. How often, on the other hand, does our horse bolt in life and how often do we fall off and have to climb on again and impose our will on it! This phase of life is described by Rudolf Steiner as the phase of the sentient soul. It is characterized by the ups and downs of life. Once again we depend on our environment, not in a physical way, as in the first seven-year-period, but in the soul sphere. The opinions of others matter to us. What do our parents-in-law think of us? How do we maintain the image of the good son or daughter with our parents?

This is a time in which we easily assume all kinds of roles — occupational roles which compensate to a certain extent our insecurity at work, family roles such as that of the good husband or wife. We ask ourselves: What is expected of a good mother or father? Here the danger exists that the roles we have assumed will suffocate our maturing 'I.' The struggle with roles — C.G. Jung designates the role as persona — which starts in this time can sometimes last a lifetime. An external lifestory begins to stand in opposition to our inner lifestory. We have to learn to reconcile them.

The fourth seven-year-period is also the time when friendships and groups are formed. We want to bring something into existence with people who think like us, or spend our spare time with many friends. In work we learn from experience, frequently change jobs, and want to see the result of our work. How happy the doctor who has assisted the birth of eight babies in a day! The doctor's 'I' grows and is strengthened. How unhappy, in contrast, the worker at the production line whose hands are empty at the end of the day! There is only one escape route by which he can compensate for the void: lots of beer or 'caipirinha' (spirit made from sugar cane). He spends hours in the pub and pretends that the emptiness does not exist.

There is great dependence on the environment, on other people, on fellow staff or on the boss at work, on our partner at home. Often we choose a partner with abilities which we do not ourselves possess and hope thereby to complement our own being. We easily develop a great dependence on our partner since in a sense we are only halves of a whole. The individualization process does not begin until the next phase from 28 to 35. Then we become whole human beings and are able to love our partner in a new way as well, without demands and dependency.

We are inspired by youthful enthusiasm, vitality; we are full of idealism and believe during this time that everything is possible, that we can succeed in everything we do. A woman, for instance, who is married to an alcoholic believes firmly that she can reform him. Another person might believe that he can introduce alternative medicine or organic food to the whole population. We thirst for knowledge and sparkle with intelligence. Not until we reach the age of 27 does the force of our enthusiasm begin to wane a little. Nowadays there are many people whose enthusiasm turns to depression which might last for several years.

This was not really the case in the lifestory of the young medical student, although the course of his life took a surprising turn in later years which was not evident from earlier developments. How did his lifestory continue? The young medical student got his doctor's diploma and specialized in psychiatry. The town in which he lived became too small for him, although he came from an even smaller town in the interior of Brazil. He went to São Paolo and he loved the city with all its adventures. His relationships slowly became firmer and he developed deeper friendships only with men. He worked in the anthroposophical clinic in São Paolo and was very interested in group work and social education. At about the age of 33 he attended a three-month course at the 'Centre of Social Development' in England. He also visited several European cities. All of this was very difficult for him, for he basically remained the simple young man from the Brazilian interior. His soul was gentle and sensitive. He was a good doctor, dealing mainly with psychological cases. He always travelled alone.

When he was approximately 36 years old, it was clear that he was going through serious inner conflicts. But when he was asked about it he always said that everything was all right. On one occasion he went hiking and became lost in the fog and woods. For three days he roamed about in the wilderness until he returned home. He refused to talk with anyone about his experiences, which must have been terrible. He began to regain his strength, but after three weeks he took an overdose of sleeping pills and medicine and went to sleep for ever — and thus the conflicts with which he lived also remained a riddle.

If we succeed in building firm ground under our feet during the phase of the sentient soul (i.e. from 21 to 28), we build the foundations for the development of our personality in subsequent years. A good boss who reviews our work with us from time to time can help us to find a healthy basis in our work. Schooling our objectivity is also helpful. I begin to learn that my point of view is not the only correct one. Objects look different, depending on the point from where I look at them, and I have to learn to observe things from a higher vantage point. A whole science exists today which is based on a Goethean phenomenological perspective and which can help young people to train their objectivity.

The twenty-eighth year: Crisis of lost abilities

Albert Einstein was once asked: 'What is genius?' He answered: 'Ninety percent perspiration and ten percent inspiration.'

This statement applies mainly to the time after the age of 28, for until then we are supported by the youthful powers of our body and intelligence and enthusiasm give flight to the whole of our being. Too many young poets, musicians and so on bury the gifts of their genius from that time onwards. A singer, for example, participated at one of our lifestory courses. But her husband had ridiculed her each time that she practised until she became so tired of it that she stopped singing. Some of the other course participants heard her singing in the bath — she was already over sixty at the time. All of them were smitten. But this happened only once. Our singer had buried her extraordinary talent and no longer dared to touch it.

A short letter from a former participant at a lifestory course:

I occasionally read my notes from your lifestory course and find a great deal confirmed. I will be 28 in December and notice quite clearly how the things which required no effort and worked almost by themselves have turned into the exact opposite. How can one deal with this knowledge in the light of the question: What can I do?

The answer is: As soon as we ask the question 'What can I do?' 'How can I apply my knowledge in a practical way?' the first step along the right path has already been taken. Because we overcome passivity, depression even, by action. This path is, of course, different for everyone.

An encounter with someone who truly shares our destiny can have a very vitalizing effect. We find ourselves again in the image of the other. New powers can arise. It is like mixing two colours together — blue and yellow make green.

What is a relationship? We can exist in parallel in a common relationship. We do much with one another and think that we understand one another well. But each person remains within his colour. The creative process has not started yet. Only when we have the courage to mix our colours, to try and understand the other person even if he or she is completely different from ourselves, only then does the creative process start and all shades can be created. There are certainly times when the blue has to be completely isolated in itself and the yellow has to shine out on its own — but in between there are all kinds of different shades of green from the rich green of the tropical forest to the delicate green of a spring meadow.

Each person has his own rhythm when walking. Walking is also an image for the course of a person's life. It is very important that each person should find his or her own rhythm in life. It is equally important to respect the rhythm of the other. But there are times when we want to walk together. What does that require? The one person perhaps running ahead while the other hobbles along behind? No, a common rhythm needs to be found. If the slower person adapts his pace to that of the fast one he will soon become tired. If the faster person fits in with the slower one he will feel as if he is stagnating and not advancing properly. A third rhythm has to be found. This is a new creative process. We face a void in this respect, we feel doubt and fear — can we succeed in building a bridge and crossing it?

Fertilization provides us with an archetypal image of a relationship. Fertilization takes place when a sperm cell meets an egg cell. If it is unsuccessful, then both egg cell and the sperm cell die. The same applies to our relationships. As long as we fertilize one another something new is created in a relationship and it blossoms!

Thus an encounter in this phase can produce many new elements and help to mitigate the feeling of helplessness in relation to our ability to develop our life. We do not, then, experience the crisis at around age 28 quite so intensely.

But every crisis can also lead to a new awakening. A good friend of mine, for example, had become a complete atheist by the time he was 28. As a child he had spent his holidays with many strictly Protestant families. Later he developed a strong aversion to religion. An older colleague once asked him whether he believed in anything. 'No,' he answered vehemently, 'and if I met Christ in the street I would spit in his face.' That made his colleague laugh a great deal. 'Then you are beyond all help,' he had to admit. Another colleague of the two was in the room and had listened to the conversation. She returned later with Rudolf Steiner's book *Occult Science* and gave it to the young unbeliever. He read the book with great enthusiasm and found many new thoughts for his life. His life had been newly fertilized by anthroposophy. His family, too, gained a new perspective. My friend continued to work diligently as a machine engineer and progressed in his career over the following years. His life took a new turn at 37 when he changed his job and devoted himself to development work in the human and business sphere.

Many people encounter inner divisions at around the age of 28. I am thinking here, for example, of the conflict facing a woman of 28. She is single with a small daughter. She has to make a decision whether to continue her life in Brazil or in Europe. She describes her situation in the following poem.

If I stay here things will go well for me.
Sometimes I see myself as two
and do not yet know
which person
I can or want to be.
(That is why I am here.)
I am well off
but I am frightened to consider the present moment
for I am divided and fear
that this split will survive me
in the next seven years.
Now is the time to choose:

which country,
which culture,
which world will I select,
plant my seeds in or maintain?
To stay in Brazil means continuing
to plant my fields of images and consciousness,
I will write and carry out my work in
information technology, the press and communications,
harvesting the fruits of what I have built up
in me and around me.
My home, my relationship to my daughter,
the secret of my books,
the emotions I feel with my records, with music
    (my culture),
which I love,
with my language
with my country which perhaps needs me more
than the world out there.
I need myself,
and if I leave, it means
planting a new country in myself,
giving everything up,
living far away.
Rebuilding in and around myself:
a new home,
a new soul,
new experiences;
touching an old dream anew,
entering uncertainty and loneliness,
an inner investment,
and the material fear
of returning a failure,
torn out of the rules of the game
which apply in Brazil.
Learning new things,
extending my cultural horizon and my consciousness,

is only worrying if there is a need
to earn money.
I have already earned money by myself.
(It was a struggle to be father and mother at the same
    time.)
And now?
Do I want more?
Can I do more?
I am well off.
Why this decision at a time when
everything appears to be settling down?
I do not understand,
why this doom?
Why a new transformation?
Who do I want to be, who can I be?
I could be well off
on every path I follow,
no matter which.
But I do not know
whether I can,
whether I want
– to be.

From 28 to 35: 'Death and resurrection'

Don't look what others do,
So many of them around,
You'll end up playing a game
Which never knows its bounds.
Just follow the path of God,
All other guides abhor,
A straight road you will walk
With others or alone.

Christian Morgenstern

To begin with, let us attempt to describe the fifth seven-year-period on the basis of a number of drawings and statements. Figure 3 (p.71) and the associated description explains the position at this age:

I am in a cave and carry a shield which I use to defend myself. But the shield is so large that I cannot see the light outside the cave. Finally, I decided to leave the cave, grasp the sword of light and fight. I was about 32 when I succeeded in taking that step.

This image and description comes from a Norwegian woman who had a happy childhood in Norway until she was 21. When she became acquainted with her present husband, a Brazilian, they decided to marry and emigrate to Brazil. The woman had great difficulty in settling down in Brazil, where she lived on a farm. She always compared the country with Norway. The sun was too hot and shone for too long. She missed the snow and the pines and the mountains. She had difficulty in learning the new language. In the meantime she became the mother of three healthy children. The woman lived completely for her family and children and her husband was her protector. She was frightened of conflict, forming friendships, and taking an active part in society. This situation lasted until she was 32. The drawing expresses this inner situation.

At 35, this woman decided to become active as a teacher on the farm. Although she still does not feel completely at home, she has grasped her work and sees new opportunities.

Now a second image (Figure 4):

I feel that I am in a cave (a) and do not notice that I am looking at and walking towards the back of the cave. I did not notice that the light was coming from behind. Suddenly I had an encounter, a conversation, and noticed that I simply needed to turn around. There I saw the light in front of me outside the cave. But first I still had to pass through a large swamp which swallowed me up to above the knees (b). Now (I am 30 years old) my experience is that I am still in the cave (c) but already nearer the entrance and I can see the light. The idea of death is familiar to me. At 12 I dreamt that I would die when I was 32 years old. Now I am beginning to learn about the whole of the human being and humankind through this lifestory course and understand the way in which death and life are linked. Before I saw no motivation or meaning in life.

This same person wrote the following poem:

I dreamt, dreamt, dreamt
for several nights — without remembering.
Today I have remembered:
I am a prisoner
in a high block of flats,
it is high and enclosed.
Someone is with me.
Up there, through the window,
I see the free world, down there.
But I cannot participate in it.
When I try to run away
I think that the punishment of twenty-four hours
will never end.
Four months have already passed —
Shall I run away or shall I stay?
Shall I fight or wait?

Figure 3.

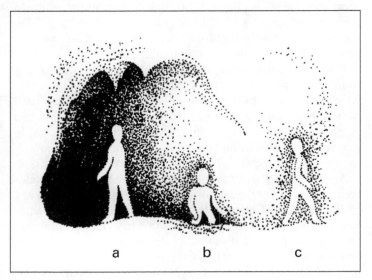

Figure 4.

What does this poem try to express?

These are images of the captive soul which cannot rise up. The past is still strongly attached and the person is wading through a swamp. He may see the light but it is still a long way off. The gifts of youth are coming to an end and his strength is waning. He has to cross the threshold — will he find the strength? Do we find the path on our own?

Many young people pass through a stage of great difficulty between the ages of 27 and 33, sometimes 35. The vital forces weaken and are used up, serious illnesses are becoming more common. Sometimes death has to be faced. Many people die before the age of 33! Cancer, traffic accidents, suicide, and so on, are typical causes of premature death.

Something new has to start at this age. The 'I' has to be strengthened and to overcome itself. The crisis which is being described here is mostly described as a crisis of talent. (The parable of the talents in the Bible makes interesting reading in this context). Do I bury the talents I have brought with me? Do I waste them? Or do I gradually transform them so that they become of use to the world from the age of 35?

The time of inspiration is past; the 'I' has to start working from the inside. What forces can help us here? The forces which are similar to our 'I,' the forces of Christ. They have flowed into humankind since the turning point of time and guide our 'I' increasingly into a individualization process, to independent decision-making capacities and our own morality. How is this possible? Many people in this phase have an encounter with a book, a philosophy or a person which guides them back to belief, back to God. The years between the age of 30 and 33, the Christ years, contain many of these elements. Some people successfully conclude this individualization process, others do not. With some it happens on a more conscious level, with others it remains in the unconscious.

If we look at Lifestory 1 (p.24) once more from this perspective, we can see that the young woman has a special experience, her dream in paradise, due to her bacillary dysentery and her high temperature. In Lifestory 2 (p.32), Tanga finds herself again through her work after two difficult years following the separation from her husband (from 30 to 32), lives with her children again and a happy phase begins. The next lifestories, too, displays these elements, a change and a turning point in life. In Lifestory 5 (p.92) a new child comes into the family which causes a change in the inner attitude of the patient. In Lifestory 6 (p.97) it is Rudolf Steiner's book *Occult Science* which introduces the new element.

But the mid-life phase from 28 to 35 has quite a different side still in many people. It is the time when our physical body is deeply penetrated by our individual self. This gives us the strength for purposeful external action and our work shows results. In this phase people are often very much oriented towards external things: establishing their careers and seeking after status, perhaps buying their first home and raising a family.

We have to develop a tolerant attitude, love and sympathy for our environment in order to balance the natural egoism of this phase. Rudolf Steiner calls this phase the time of the intellectual and sentient soul. He links these two terms quite consciously. Thinking (the intellect) and feeling (sentience) must be integrated in our personality. Those who are drawn towards thinking and will, must develop their emotional life more. Men in particular have to develop the female side of their soul or, as C.G. Jung calls it, the *anima*. In contrast, those who are drawn towards feeling, have to develop the capacities of thinking and will to a greater extent. For women this also means developing the male side of their soul or the *animus*, according to C.G. Jung.

Rudolf Treichler characterizes the years from 21 to 28 as: 'How do I experience the world?' He places the phase from 28 to 35 under the motto: 'How is the world organized — and how do I organize myself in this relationship with the world?' We have to learn to find the proper interaction with our environment. It is important to find the right balance between family and work — to become adaptable on the one hand, but not to allow my 'I' to be suffocated by my environment on the other, so that I can develop freely as an individual. We become less dependent on our partners — we become ourselves to a greater extent and can thus develop our capacity to love. Marriage can turn into real friendship in which each person respects the personality of the other and does not constantly make demands. If someone does a physically demanding job then this is the time when they reach peak fitness. That is something which can be observed in many sports. Moreover, people develop an extraordinary organizational ability in the years from 28 to 35 and have a tendency to lay plans for the future.

The fifth seven-year-period is the phase when we are able to create a balance between the idealism and easy disillusionment of the time from 21 to 28 and the materialism and sclerotization of the years from 35 to 42.

Lifestory 3: Experiences between 28 and 35

I don't know where to start. I cannot, of course, say that everything started at 30. That would be untrue. There were thirty years before then which were a preparation for what was to follow.

A family. Father, mother, three daughters. I was the middle daughter. A Jewish family. My father, born in Russia, had emigrated to Brazil with his parents at the age of eight. They were weighed down with persecution, anti-Semitism, poverty, the will and the necessity of succeeding. My mother came from a Jewish family which had lived in South America for three generations already, which was therefore very much 'assimilated.' My father, the artist, the intellectual, the businessman. My mother, the excellent housewife, the good mother, the good wife, all love, devotion, loyalty.

I think that I had a happy childhood. From an early age I learnt to win people over through my cheerful nature, humour and creativity. These qualities were highly valued in our house. That is how I avoided confrontation, arguments and irritations. I also learnt to play the game of happiness at an early age. I sought all that glitters in order to be loved. And I succeeded.

I had friends, many friends and a family which loved and admired me a great deal.

My father died when I was almost 17. That was difficult, but life went on.

I married at 20. I was in love and open for my new life. Children followed immediately. I gave birth to three children in four years. Then came a whole decade in which I devoted myself to achieving maximum perfection in order to bring up my children well, to nourish and clothe them, play and sing with them, show them affection and give them what I had received as example in my own childhood. All of this was intermingled with the wish to be 'someone' for the outside world, an artist for example, and, above all, to be 'good' in everything I did.

During this time I also encountered a new way of looking at life and the world, human beings and God. For the first time I grasped very slowly and subsequently accepted — through anthroposophy — that there is a spiritual world. Gradually I turned from a materialist into a spiritualist. For the Judaism of my father was tied to popular tradition but he was extremely materialistic and agnostic and had a great influence on me.

And then I became divided. It was difficult for me to acknowledge a spiritual world in front of my friends. It was even more difficult to acknowledge my Christianity to my Jewish family. Thus I spent ten years with two faces — or a thousand faces. I was successful in all areas of my activity without, however, putting down roots in any of them.

When I was 29 I felt very insecure and frustrated. As a woman living in this world in this century a part of me wanted to fulfil the task of mother, wife, housewife well, and no one was better at it than I. The other part of me wanted to 'be someone,' work in a profession, be acknowledged, earn money. At the same time I wanted to be charming and attractive and stop my husband ever falling out of love with me. In short, I wanted to be 'superwoman' and did not succeed. Frustration began to take hold of me while I was trying at the same time to convince myself that everything was all right.

In the year when I turned 30, my husband and I went through an enormous marriage crisis. Since it had never even remotely occurred to me that something like this could happened to me I fell from a great height into a deep hole. Fear, anxiety, insecurity took hold of me. I had to admit for the first time that I was nothing like I had imagined myself to be or, more accurately, that I was none of the things which — in my eyes — others expected me to be. I suffered deep depression and feelings of anxiety never left me. In my eyes I was nothing — as woman, mother, professional, in everything I did.

Immediately after my husband and I succeeded in rebuilding our relationship, my mother had to undergo an operation for a hysteromyoma. Her womb was removed and this made a great impression on me. I recall that I had the feeling that my first home, into which I had been born and in which I had been protected, that my 'nest' had been thrown in the bin. Now I had to rely on myself.

Less than two months later I became ill with intestinal bleeding. I was diagnosed as suffering from ulcerative reticulocolitis, a psychosomatic illness I was told. A cure was difficult on the whole. The illness was likely to develop such that the colon would have to be removed or that cancer-like swellings would form.

After a further two months my mother was diagnosed as having cancer. At that I completely lost the ground from under my feet, I no longer had anything to hold on to. But I acted as if nothing was wrong. The only thing I wanted was for the doctor to give me a drug which would hide my illness. The illness did not exist and I continued to live my life as 'superwoman' at full throttle. It was as if the illness and I were two separate beings and as if I was dragging it along beside me like a sidecar on a motorbike.

For two years we continued like this, my illness and I. When my mother died I felt that I could not bear the loss and separation. My condition became very much worse and suddenly an inner transformation took place in me. I now saw my illness as myself. I decided to acknowledge my illness and to tackle it completely on my own. I no longer went to any conventional or anthroposophical doctor and completely reversed my treatment and diet. I had acupuncture on a daily basis and no longer listened to anyone. I did not take any medicines, did not undergo any examinations and paid no attention to the bleeding and diarrhoea.

My body rapidly began to weaken. I grew thin and it became impossible for me to do anything other than take care of myself. I was no longer able to work or study, take care of the children or the house or participate in my husband's life. My life was centred only around myself, there was no middle course. Only life or death. I became so weak that I was no longer able to carry my own bag. I got arthritis in my hands, feet and knees, my ankles began to swell and I had to walk with a stick. Boils began to form all over my body due to the poisons left in my body from my colon. I had more than one hundred boils, large ones, some of them with three to seven heads. All of this was accompanied by hot flushes with temperatures of up to forty degrees. I had a great deal of pain in my body, which had already been considerable even before the deterioration of my abdominal illness. I was completely anaemic and malnourished but even then I did not want to listen to any advice. I still had much of the 'superwoman' in me and thought that I could cure myself by my own strength and with acupuncture alone.

My condition finally became so bad that I was taken to hospital in an extremely serious state. I was unable to undergo

*an operation and my recovery was very difficult because of my
extreme weakness.*

*At this moment I felt that I would die and that is also what
everyone around me assumed. I could see and feel death here
at my side. I felt that I was at the threshold, I could see the
other side, it was merely a matter of slipping over. At the
beginning I felt annoyed, even angry. I thought: Why me of all
people? I am still so young, I still want to do such a lot in life,
I have not achieved anything yet. Then I became frightened,
very frightened. Not of the moment of death as such, for I
think I had already experienced the extremes of pain. Rather,
it was fear of an absence of belief. I, who seriously believed
in the existence of a spiritual world, a God, in life after death,
in the meaningful nature of life on earth, in the development
of human beings, suddenly found myself confronted with the
fear that there would be nothing after death. And if everything
was a lie? If everything stops with death? If my whole life has
no meaning? I began to take leave of people in my thoughts
when I saw them; it could be the last time. I looked out of the
window from my bed, observed the trees, the sky, the changes
in the weather, the smells, with my eyes, ears and nose like
a person taking things in for the last time with her sensory
organs. Greedily I grasped at a word or a cuddle from my
children and husband.*

*Once I was able to respond to the state of being physically
at the limit — I was, however, still very weak — I suffered a
further setback: a medical mistake meant that I took the wrong
medicine for two weeks. This medicine caused a serious attack
of diarrhoea as well as containing a toxicological and hallu-
cinatory substance which took me to the edge of madness and
death. My pupils enlarged so that I looked inward rather than
outward and I had terrible palpations and a feeling of pins
and needles in my arms which made me feel as if death was
about to strike. As if that were not enough, I suffered a panic
reaction which triggered a feeling of shock towards everything
in my environment with hot flushes and anxieties. In addition,*

I had hallucinations which provoked further feelings of anxiety. I curled up in a foetal position and even sucked my thumb. I came very close to death, as one doctor told me. Once I again I had the experience of having encountered death at close quarters. I understand completely what it means to have a panic attack and what it means to feel completely alone in the world, isolated from other people, incapable of receiving help from others although they want to give it.

I became so introverted with physical and spiritual pain that my husband decided to put a television in my hospital room to distract me. But my perception was so finely tuned after what I had been through that I saw the television programmes with eyes which were still more open. There are always advertisements between films which offer our consumer society silly and superfluous things. This is interspersed with the news which carries willy-nilly reports — as if we were dealing with weather reports and bananas — of terrible conflicts on the other side of the world, of death, murder, revolutions, earthquakes, erupting volcanoes, car accidents, catastrophes involving ships and aircraft, terrible dramas. This is directly followed by a humorous programme with dancing girls. All of this was deeply shocking to me and for the first time I became aware — not only on an intellectual level — of what it means to be a world citizen today: all people, both those living here alongside me and those on the other side of the world, and all who lived at that particular time, were my contemporaries. We lived together on this planet at the same time. Each one with his destiny, each one bearing his cross, but all together, and in some way it was also a concern of mine what a person say in China was going through. I felt deeply that we human beings were all a limb, a foot or a head of the one single human being. And I felt that I was leaving my human family at that point in order to live another life. My life here on earth had been changed by my problems and my experiences, but also by the others. I took all of this with me.

Suddenly it dawned on me: If I was destined to survive, it could not be for nothing, given the chaos affecting humankind. There had to be a meaning to it. There had to be some purpose to my staying alive so that I would remain with everyone — whether I could reach them or not — in order to live with them, be active with them, make my contribution, my 'brush-stroke' as it were, to the great evolutionary picture of human development. I felt an immense responsibility and love inside me towards everything.

Slowly I began to react against my illness. My strength gradually increased and I had greater hope. I started to do clay modelling as a therapeutic measure and also did some gardening. After all, for someone like myself, who had been involved in an excarnation process, the earth provided the best means to find a hold, an anchor. By concerning myself with colours and shapes in a living way, I responded to my situation with something which was living. I surrounded myself with beauty.

I avoided depressing situations. I searched out everything that was beautiful and gentle. That provided me with sustenance. I had the feeling of being reborn. It was as if I had reached the bottom of a well and could now start living again. I was able to establish relationships with other people again. The need to reaffirm myself constantly through my 'success' had gone. It was now a little easier for me to say no because it was no longer necessary for me to try and please other people so that they would love me. I was happy, very happy, to be alive, to be here with the others. I began to love myself more and to accept myself without having to be 'superwoman' and I had fewer expectations of myself. I overflowed with love for humankind and for those around me. I was full of joy.

I thought of my age and made a comparison. Jesus came to mind, whose life until 30 had been in preparation of his great mission, who began his great path of suffering and renunciation at 30 and was crucified at 33 in order to be resurrected. I felt that I — of course in a completely different way — had gone through a similar experience. At 30 I had begun the difficult path in the direction of death, had suffered great physical pain, fear, panic, loneliness and weakness. I was totally dependent on others and had to accept their hand without being able to give anything in return. I had felt powerlessness and dying without it having happened properly. At 33 the fall in direction of my 'crucifixion' was practically unstoppable. Then I emerged from that as if I had been reborn. I feel that my present life is divided into a 'before' and 'after.' That is quite clear.

It went so far that I decided to take a step which is very difficult for a person of Jewish extraction like me. I decided to be baptized. With that I decided to give concrete shape here on earth, and also in the spiritual world, to the great step which I had already taken. Namely to acknowledge what had taken place in me: the perception of a spiritual world which is very strong, to which I belong, and through which I am active here on earth for as long as I am here in the community of those around me.

I am not well. This illness is very difficult to treat. But I am strong and have the energy to be active and work, to study and to be together with my family and the world. I do not want to lose that. I feel a little smaller, but perhaps — and for precisely that reason — I feel better. I no longer have such great expectations of myself but I like myself better.

I have not yet reached where I want to be. Many of the old mistakes still cling to me. Frequently I catch myself struggling unconsciously to do everything correctly come what may and often I relapse into the old pattern. Sometimes I am also afraid. But in this way I discover myself more than ever as a person in the middle of a process of development and am happy about every day which I am permitted to spend here.

Lifestory 4

At the age of 36 I am beginning to see new perspectives in life. Although I still feel fragile and have the impression that I must protect myself inwardly, I do sense significant change. My father was Brazilian, my mother Danish. Both were single children. My father married my mother because I was already on the way. My father was a handsome man, a bon vivant, and everyone admired him a great deal. My mother, in contrast, was introverted and full of complexes. She was very strict and lived an orthodox life by all the norms. I spent my childhood partly in Brazil but every year I was allowed to travel to Denmark for a few months, where I lived with my grandparents. The first time that I went to Denmark — and this is also my first memory — I was two years old. Here in Brazil I went to a small kindergarten. My sister was born when I was two-and-a-half years old and I remember feeling very jealous during my mother's pregnancy. I had mumps as a child and my tonsils were removed. I also suffered insomnia due to feelings of anxiety.

I started school at six. I felt very insecure and was jealous of the other children. I began to read and then also fell in love platonically for the first time. My parents separated when I was seven. Until then I was a bed wetter. I stayed with my mother. She remarried when I was eight. This second marriage only lasted four years. My father dominated my mother, was full of energy but immature. He was jealous of me and my sister. I saw my father in the Club on Sundays, but he did not bother much with me. The only time he made something of an effort was when I had measles at nine.

From 15 to 17, then, I spent every summer holiday in Denmark with my grandparents where I felt at home and contented. At nine I packed my suitcase and wanted to leave home. I felt alone and very frustrated. We went to live somewhere else after my mother had separated from her second husband. *My mother thought that I was very egotistical; I felt a heavy burden on me. My mother began to drink shortly after her separation from her second husband. But I only noticed it when I was 13 because she drank secretly. At 13 I wanted to stay at a boarding school in Denmark. I spent a whole year there. It was a beautiful time. I experienced warmth and love and had many friends. I learnt to speak Danish, English and German, and also to knit and do embroidery.*

At 14 I returned to a Brazilian school. I was never emotionally close to my father. I learnt during this time to look happy on the outside. Everything appeared to be fine but inside I suffered anxiety, sadness, apprehension. I wanted to attract the attention of others. I had my first boyfriend at 15 and a second one at 16, with whom I had sexual relations for the first time. This created a tremendous feeling of guilt in me. Both my grandparents in Denmark died when I was 17. When my mother discovered that I was no longer a virgin at 17, my feelings of guilt grew still stronger. My mother told me: 'You have stabbed me in the back.' I had to stay at home for a month as punishment. In the same year my father hit me in the face for misbehaviour. These events made any feelings of sexual desire in me disappear.

At 17 I travelled to Europe with my sister. My mother drank a lot during that time and wanted to commit suicide. I became acquainted with my second boyfriend and my attitude to my sexuality returned to normal. My mother said of me that I did these things in order to draw attention to myself and attract men, but this friend did not reciprocate my love. I caught gonorrhoea at 18. My mother said: 'Your friend does not respect you.' At 19 I went to university and studied tourism. I also travelled to Denmark and the north-east of Brazil with my sister. For the first time I had a good relationship with my sister. At 20 I became acquainted with my third boyfriend, who was a difficult person; it ended with him attacking me physically. I sought help and protection from my father but he did not help me although he knew the friend well. This experience of my

*father was a great disappointment to me. And my mother, who
was very physically disposed, could not stand seeing the same
traits in her daughter.*

*I knew that I had a great deal of potential but I was still
lacking in self-confidence. I ended the relationship with my
third boyfriend when I was 22 and shortly afterwards began
a friendship with my present husband. But I sensed that my
husband's family did not accept me but rejected me. I reacted
with aggression and thought that this was connected with my
mother. I was also embarrassed by my mother, who continued
her drinking. She finally went to the United States, settled
there and only came to Brazil once a year. This was a great
relief to me. I began the preparations for my marriage, but had
no money and had to do everything myself. Both my mother
and my mother-in-law were absent.*

*At 26 I gave birth to my first daughter. The period during
which I nursed my child was a good time; she gave me great
pleasure. I tried to provide her with whole food as best I could.
My mother-in-law made fun of me but I nevertheless felt like a
'supermum.' But the relationship with my husband, including
sexual relations, was difficult. My interest had waned and I
always felt guilty and a bad person and thought that my husband was the good one. Thus I finally decided at 27 to go into
therapy. Here I discovered how my present life with my husband was a repetition of what I had practised during my youth.
I always tried to conjure up a crisis in order then to be able to
enjoy the reconciliation. I felt dissatisfied if the days remained
the same and nothing new happened. As a young couple we
really lived beyond our means. At 28 I had a minor affair and
wanted to separate from my husband, but soon recognized that
my place was at home and that I had to fight for my marriage.
At the same time I came across meditation techniques and
also began to develop an interest in spiritual reading matter. I
began yoga exercises as well. In that year a visit by my mother
helped me a great deal in the reconciliation with my husband.*

At 29 I became pregnant again. It was an exhausting time

for we were converting the house at the same time which cost me a lot of strength. I also felt that my mother-in-law was interfering a great deal in family matters. I did not really assert myself as wife and housewife but always stood aside. My son was born when I was 30. The doctor thought that he might be suffering from diabetes. I was very weak and was confined to bed for a whole month. Shortly afterwards the doctor diagnosed hypertony in my son. Was it my fault, was it shock? I felt very insecure, threatened and could not articulate my feelings. Sometimes mortal fear even took hold of me and I tried to become harder towards the outside. I did not recover properly and at 31 I was finally diagnosed as diabetic. I wanted nothing to do with medicines but became very embarrassed because I was not perfect. I stopped smoking, which I had begun at an early age. I did not admit that I was ill and refused all treatment. I noticed how I controlled and manipulated the relationship with my husband; the same situation repeated itself which I had used at home with my mother and her alcoholism. Something had to change. I lost 14 kg of weight and my physical condition was very bad. My mother invited me to the States and I flew there with the child. She prepared a lovely reception for me and we were finally able to be reconciled. I began to accept my illness, was prescribed Insulin and my condition began to improve significantly. It was as if my mother wanted to make up during that time what she had neglected to do during my youth. She cared for me in a very loving way.

After I returned to Brazil from the US, my husband's family also accepted me better. From that time onwards I felt that I had been reborn and that my mother's pregnancy when she was carrying me was properly concluded only now.

At 33 I organized a birthday party for myself for the first time, invited people, and my hypertonic child slowly began to walk.

At 34 I opened a boutique which I ran for one and a half years. I had a business partner to begin with but she stopped and the work was too much for me alone.

At 35 I took part in a lifestory course in 'Artemisia' for the first time. In addition, I read a book by Luise Ray which was very important to me.

My mother-in-law was very critical, as always, but I had the strength to stand up to her. I also attended an 'Alanon' group of where relatives of alcoholics can talk. There I discovered a lot about the psychology of my behaviour. At 35 I realized that I was master of my destiny and also that I was able to heal myself. Sexual relations with my husband improved. My husband developed both in his professional and personal life; he also went into therapy. I was generally happier and we were able to spend lovely holidays together as a family.

Some additional notes concerning my lifestory:
I am left-handed and was never corrected. I always felt myself to be an outsider and was incapable of fitting in with a group. I was shy and jealous at the same time. My main feelings were frustration, bitterness, being hurt very easily, and I was full of resentment. During my youth I put great store by values and was also very aggressive. A further characteristic of my life is that I moved a lot and undertook many journeys between Brazil and Denmark.

This lifestory leaves one with a sense that the crisis between the ages of 30 and 33 was successfully overcome. Here too this person came very close to death in order then to arise and be resurrected. It was an essential element that the mother of the patient repeated, as it were, the process of pregnancy and caring love. This led to reconciliation between mother and daughter. At the same time the daughter was able to free herself from the personality of her mother who had exercised such a decisive influence on her life. From the age of 35 onwards her own impulse came increasingly to the fore. Where does this impulse lead? We will concern ourselves with this question in the next chapter.

The thirty-fifth year and the phase from 35 to 42

If I believe that I am what
this world makes of me, there is nothing I can do.
In such a situation I will not, of course, be able to prevent
the destruction of the planet.
But if I think what originally
each one of us is, or could be –
independently of the world situation –
namely an autonomous human being,
responsible to the world and for the world, then
there is, of course, a great deal I can do.

Vaclav Hável

We have survived the difficult years which we live through
from 30 to 33 and enter our thirty-fifth year. From a certain
perspective we are now poised at the midway point of our life.
We have descended most deeply into our incarnation; we are in
closest proximity to the earth. Now we begin to free ourselves
from our body again and strive upwards. The phases of our life
up to that point were like a deep breath taking in the cosmos,
nature, our environment, education, knowledge and so on.
Gradually we feel secure and at home in our work and home
environment. We are able increasingly to realize on earth what
we have brought with us in our 'I' as intentions, motifs and mis-
sions from the sphere before birth. We make increasing use of
our inner resources, of the capabilities which we have brought
with us or acquired. And we are sure of our path of further
development. The Christ forces which we have assimilated in
the previous seven-year-period help us to develop true brotherli-
ness, tolerance and respect towards other people.

But the life phase which we have entered also has its negative aspects: We can become great egotists and dictators at
this age. Every person's biographical development contains

the danger that he or she may turn into a mini Napoleon. (Napoleon crowned himself at 35!) We have to fight against egotism during this time and in this, too, we are helped by tolerance and a positive attitude towards others. In many lectures, Rudolf Steiner speaks of the things which are only able to come to appearance after the age of 35. For example, people only become capable of judgement when their deeds and thoughts are of use to the world. A receptive attitude gradually turns into one which gives to the world. Our spirit is no longer concerned with our physical and soul development. It is increasingly liberated to strive into the future.

The American journalist Gail Sheehy calls this phase the authenticity crisis or the phase of the demystification of our dreams. We have to dismantle the illusions which we have about ourselves. We have to ask ourselves: What would remain of us if we abandoned all our roles? The maturing of our individuality means that we no longer want to live for appearances, but for reality. In a relationship, for example, I no longer do certain things because I feel duty-bound to do them because my role as a man or woman demands it, but for love. It is also easier for me to say no. The answer does not have to be yes only because others expect it; I would only become upset afterwards about doing something only because that is what is expected. I act from conviction and on the basis of my authentic self. A small example: When I was 26 to 28 and had just started practising as a doctor, I was embarrassed to meet my patients when I was doing the weekly shopping. I preferred to send my domestic for the messages. From 35 onwards, I remember, I had great pleasure in going to the market. It was a real joy to select the best and most nourishing fruit and vegetables. I was no longer bothered in the least if I met patients while doing this. I had broken through to an authentic approach, to a love of what I was doing, which made it irrelevant what others thought about me.

The Freemasons express this dismantling of a falsely built up personality in the symbol of the hammer.

We are now living in the phase which Rudolf Steiner called

the phase of the consciousness soul. We observe things in a clearer and more critical fashion. The danger exists, however, that our life becomes nothing more than habit and frequently we experience a feeling of emptiness. Courage is required at this point to turn 'outwardly-directed criticism' into 'inwardly directed criticism.' Each person must ask him or herself: What are my limits? Where do my capacities and opportunities for action lie? At the age from 21 to 28 we think that nothing is impossible. I might marry a man who is an alcoholic, convinced that I am strong enough to stop him drinking. Or I have the idea of working in the cause of an ecological world and am certain that everyone will take up and accept my ideas.

Now, in this period, I am confronted with my limits. It is not possible to achieve everything and I am able to realize only certain parts of myself. I must not overvalue myself. 'Not I, but Christ in me' — this knowledge grows into a spiritual reality.

On the one hand, then, we have a tendency to overvalue ourselves. On the other hand there are many people — mainly women who were perhaps intensively involved in bringing up a family and educating their children in the preceding years — who believe that they have learned nothing and did no proper work, and who underestimate their creative capacities. There is thus also a tendency in the opposite direction, to undervalue one's capabilities. It is up to the individual to look back once more: What intentions did I leave behind by way of impulses, professional ambitions? How can I reactivate these elements?

We have now reached the age of 37 — the time of the second lunar node. Here the impulse to make a new start is even stronger than at the first lunar node at 18½. We experience an impulse to leave the past behind us and the urge to adopt new values, new standards. Many people change their jobs or return to university at this point in order to begin to complete their life's task.

Those who have become accustomed to paying attention to their dreams feel the need to change something in their life.

And they feel that they now have the ability to do so. Erich
Fromm characterized these states of soul in terms of being and
having: The having phase is finished; I *have* a wife, I *have* a
family, I *have* a job, I *have* a home, sometimes I even *have* a
factory already. But does that mean anything? Perhaps I have
lost a lot in the process of acquisition: the contact with my
children, the contact with my wife, the harmony of my real
values. Often these inner conflicts become apparent to me and
I want to change something. A new direction is in the process
of developing which I want to give my life after 40.

Most people also encounter the question of death in this
phase. We begin to decline physically. This is expressed in
dreams about dying and feelings of fear about death. Typical
statements in these years are: 'I sometimes think that I do not
have much longer to live.' 'My father died at 42 and I will
not become much older than that either.' Or something happens which is similar to the case when a woman came to my
surgery and said: 'I don't know what's wrong with me. I am
suddenly afraid to cross the road.' In response to my question: 'How old are you?' she answered: 'I have just turned
38.' Such experiences and others reflect the influence and the
experience of death. It is as if the angel of death is looking
across from the other side, from the end of my life and says to
me: Reflect on what you still want to do in the coming years,
what you have neglected and what you still want to transform
into deeds.

C.G. Jung characterizes this time as the phase of the 'great
death.' On a soul level it is the expression of casting off that
part of ourselves which is directed towards external things on
the one hand, and of the deteriorating powers of the physical
body on the other.

A new interest in spiritual matters comes alive in Tanga
(Lifestory 2, p.32), for instance, at the age of 37 — a seed
which her grandmother planted in her in her early childhood.

Here is another statement, made by a 37-year-old woman
during an assessment of a lifestory course:

I have now discovered that I myself am the hero of my life-story. For the whole of my life I sought the hero outside and now this lifestory course has made me see that she is really inside.

The experience of death such as we have described it is triggered by the degenerative processes in the organism which now rise from the physical body into consciousness. But it also allows for a considerable expansion of consciousness. We begin to see the source of things. We are now in a position to distinguish what is important from what is unimportant. Often we have spiritual experiences. We might hear the 'sun resounding' at sunset, or, in observing a blossom, we might suddenly understand the nature of life. Our relationships with other people can also deepen. We succeed in getting away from our egotism and in perceiving the true being of the other person. The 'little prince' in the other person is revealed in his greatness. If we understand the essential nature of a person or an idea, we can stay true to it. A phase of great spiritual uplift begins. Our words increasingly gain life experience and life content.

We may also, however, gloss over our inner emptiness during this phase of life. We try to escape from ourselves, avoid confronting ourselves by indulging in alcohol or cocaine. Many people also face the danger of succumbing to materialism and wanting to possess ever more — by founding one business after another for example — and continuing to see the meaning of life in piling up ever more material goods.

The following lifestory of a 42-year-old man takes our reflections on the laws of biographical development up to the age of 42 a stage further.

Lifestory 5

I am the third son of a Dutch farming family. My two elder siblings are also boys and there are several more after me. I grew up in Holland until I was 14. I used to trot along behind my brothers when we went to school. They thought it very funny when I was left behind along the way and finally stood there alone. Our family was Catholic and we said the rosary every evening at home. Our childhood was relatively harmonious on the whole. Nevertheless, my mother had little time for us and we had to help our father a lot in the fields.

When I was 14, the whole family emigrated to Brazil. We were given a whole new set of clothes for our departure. It turned out that these clothes were totally useless in Brazil because of the heat and frequent rain. At 15 I fell ill with hepatitis.

I had to plough with horses and plant maize and cotton, vegetables and tomatoes. In Holland we had grown nothing but flowers. Soon my family bought a tractor which only my two elder brothers were allowed to use, however. For many years we worked without holidays. At 17 I became seriously poisoned by agro-chemicals and spent a month in hospital with damaged kidneys.

At 19, when on one occasion I went for a drive in our small van, I was a little late in coming back and my brother became very angry. My father encouraged him further: 'Teach him a lesson!' That hurt me a great deal. My two brothers and myself were always engaged in a sort of competition among ourselves. I always got on very badly with my two elder brothers. In contrast, I had a very good relationship with my younger brother. But he soon left home to go to university and so I lost a friend. My father always protected my elder brothers. My oldest brother was the only one he listened to. I, on the other hand, always had to fight for my position. When my oldest brother married, my father came into our bedroom on the eve of the wedding — we three brothers all slept in the same room — in order to say goodbye to him. He told him that he was his favourite child. That was very painful for me.

My second brother was also married already when I married at 24. But all three of us continued to work in my father's company. It was a family business which was integrated into a larger Dutch colony comprising several farms. My father was intent on building up the best and largest business.

My marriage was a good one, but we were unable to have any children of our own. So we adopted a boy when I was 28 and a girl when I was 30. At 31 I fell in love with a secretary in the company. A very difficult situation arose, as my wife was very jealous although no intimate relations developed between me and the secretary. She remained some months longer in our company. When I was 33, we decided to adopt a third child in order to overcome our marriage difficulties. It was as if the three adoptions were decreed by fate.

All these emotional difficulties resulted in my developing a melanoma which had to be removed. Shortly after that I began an anthroposophical course of treatment.

The company grew bigger and bigger and we began to specialize in flowers, mainly gladioli and chrysanthemums. Today it is a business with seven hundred employees. Flowers give me great pleasure.

At 37 I developed a small skin carcinoma on my chest which had to be removed.

From the age of 35 onwards I felt greater inner freedom. I also began to give my life a different meaning and greater value. My father withdrew from the business when I was 40 and my elder brother became president.

I sense that I have difficulty in dealing with my children as a father, but I make a great effort to do so properly. That is probably linked to the fact that the relationship between me and my father was such a difficult one and that it was very hard for me to establish a rapport with him.

I was 41 the first time I took part in a lifestory course. My

*relationship with my wife became more and more difficult.
My interest in anthroposophy grew stronger and stronger. My
wife had been brought up very strictly Catholic. She controlled
me and the children very strongly. I felt that I had to work
more intensively on my lifestory and on an understanding of
the course of my life. A lecture at a lifestory course, based on
Karl König's book* Brothers and Sisters, *gave me an insight
into the life situation of my first, second and third brothers. I
also learnt a number of things about my third adopted child,
with whom I identify a great deal. In this way I also became
aware that it was possible for me to introduce some new elements into our relationships. I attended a second lifestory
course. I am also beginning to understand the relationship
with my two elder brothers more clearly now.*

*I fell very deeply in love once more at the age of 42, and
even thought about a separation from my wife and making a
new start which might bring me a new impetus for the next
stage in my life. I thought about this very intensively for a
whole year but remained true to my principles and my family.
Basically I know that change has to come from the inside, not
the outside.*

The crisis at the age of 42

The forty-second year marks a turning point in a person's
lifestory. People's development in the next three seven-year-
periods from 42 to 63 depends largely on the transformation
which has taken place within them. The forty-second year
might be described as an existential crisis. It cannot, of course,
be pinned down exactly to that year. For some people the critical phase starts as early as the late thirties and with others it
extends far into the next seven-year-period.

In my own lifestory I had the feeling of entering a dark
tunnel. I knew well that there would be light at the other end
of the tunnel but it nevertheless took several years, to the age

of 45, until I re-emerged from this condition. Two images describe the feeling which a person has during this phase of their life:

It is as if one is immersed in a deep well with the feeling of not being able to get out any longer. Often one has to allow oneself to fall to the bottom in order to be able to push oneself off the bottom and start the ascent. If we look back on our lifestory, we will see that there were always people who helped us to cope with difficult situations. From this point onwards we have to do that ourselves. We have to give ourselves a hand, as it were. No one helps us out of the well, only we ourselves. That gives us a certain feeling of impotence.

Another comparison: You are walking through a tropical jungle. The path goes through undergrowth, prickly bushes, liana, and other obstacles. Suddenly it emerges at the summit of a mountain. There you experience for the first time the magnificent landscape which surrounds you and you begin to understand it as a whole. Why does the river meander like that over there? Because the land is very flat. And over there a mighty waterfall is being born. You can make many more such discoveries.

We have to learn to read this mighty landscape which we survey. We begin to observe and understand the landscape of our life from a higher vantage point.

The so-called 'mid-life crisis,' which is so often referred to today, is closely linked to the values and views which a person has developed in the preceding consciousness soul phase. The crisis may be delayed well into the forties with men who are completely caught up in their external work, their career and their success. They continue to strive for success, for higher status. This prevents the transformation taking place which represents the task of the next phase. Often the result is increasing dissatisfaction which may end in depression. This crisis at the age of 42 could be equated with the 'mid-life crisis.' But we should not overlook, as we said above, that it may occur at an earlier stage in some people and a later one in others.

Career women are affected in a similar way to success-oriented men. But women who were looking after children and a family until then are particularly affected by the critical life situation in the forty-second year. Frequently they suffer tremendously from such a crisis and rebel against the constraints of their life. But the major task for each individual consists of transforming their personal business and their life situation from the inside — that is something which we would describe as inner maturity. It should be achieved at this point.

The author of Lifestory 5 clearly experiences that the change must come from inside. But many people do not recognize that. They experience a great emptiness and attempt to deceive themselves that this is not so by throwing themselves into their work, or by sex or alcohol.

We only reach real maturity in life, the full awareness of our 'I,' at 42. At 21 we were only partially adults, at 42 we are full adults. Life has matured us — events in our life have ripened into fruits if they have been transformed and integrated into our personality. Now we can use in increasing measure the maturity we have acquired for the benefit of others.

The dying processes which started in the previous phase of life still echo in the soul and allow us to sense what the 'great death,' as C.G. Jung calls it, means. We have to ask ourselves: What elements in us can we allow to die? What should be revitalized or, indeed, encouraged to grow?

The values which we have re-acquired in the age of the consciousness soul, that is, in the period from 35 to 42, are now consolidated. We come to terms with the mistakes which our parents made in bringing up their children. We can forgive our parents and create a new relationship with them. Anyone who still blames their parents or education has not developed in life, or has stopped developing.

At around the age of 40, Rudolf Steiner tells us, we cross the threshold. What does that mean, 'crossing the threshold'? It means that experiences of a spiritual kind spontaneously occur in people. That is connected with the liberation of vital forces which were tied to the organs up to that point. From the age of 35, the 'I' slowly begins to separate itself from the organic forces which it played a part in forming and moulding. These forces enter our consciousness and can overwhelm us. Today it is important that we cross the threshold with growing awareness. Many people have threshold experiences ever more frequently — not only in this phase of life, but in other years as well. If we are not up to these experiences, they can lead to psychological disorders and mental illness. But if we succeed in handling them in the right way they can enrich our life. And they can confirm the existence of a spiritual world.

The following lifestory highlights some aspects and peculiarities which are characteristic of the phase from 35 to 42. It is written by a 57-year-old woman.

Lifestory 6

I was born in the interior of the state of São Paolo. My father was Brazilian, my mother was of Spanish descent. My father was chief of police. He often took me along on his motorcycle. I am the third child in a family of four children — I have an elder brother and two sisters. I was born after my mother had seven miscarriages after the birth of her second child. I was already walking at nine months. We had a large house with many animals, monkeys, crocodiles, and so on. At the age of three-and-a-half I fell ill with bacillary dysentery.

At four I started going to a Catholic kindergarten. I defended my elder brother, who was weaker than I was. My father had many other women and I often saw my mother crying. At approximately six years of age I went fishing with my father and fell into the water. I remember that I had a darkness-lightness experience as I went under.

At seven I went to school. I was a good pupil. I did not enjoy playing with dolls, I tore out their hair and turned them into men. *My first platonic love occurred at nine with a child from the neighbourhood. My tonsils were removed in the same year. Before that I had had measles. We moved to another town when I was ten. Once again we had a big house and I helped my mother a great deal with baking biscuits and bottling fruit and vegetables. I had to repeat a year at school in the new town. I remember from that time that I looked at flowers and asked myself questions such as: Where do the colour and the scent come from? How do the seasons come about? Also, I constantly measured myself against my elder sister. I started menstruating at ten.*

We always spent our holidays on farms. At 13 I started to play basketball. My father forbade me to do it and I secretly escaped through the window. Finally, my father heard my name on the radio during a competition and then my parents allowed me to play after all. At 14 I began to play at theatre and wrote some small pieces — that too was forbidden by my father. I fell ill with chickenpox at the same time.

I joined the Catholic youth movement and also participated in gospel groups. Similarly, I edited a newspaper; I wanted to make Christ accessible to people. I fell in love with my teachers on a number of occasions. Atomic theory interested me during that time. I was also interested in the stars and philosophy. I had my first experience of death at 17. A female and a male friend died a short time one after the other. Those losses were very close to my heart. Thus I began to ask about the nature of death.

As early as 14 and 15, and particularly at 18, I experienced my muscles, felt them intensely and was interested in gymnastics and movement of every kind. In the same year, at 18, I fell ill with mumps. My parents moved to São Paolo during this time and I remained in the interior of the country. I played in a basketball team which called itself 'The Black Panther.' I studied hard and took seven subjects in one year. At 19 I also moved to São Paolo. I suffered a serious allergy at the time.

I really wanted to study philosophy. My teacher advised

against it, however, and suggested that I should go to sports college. I had to sit a test for admission to sports college which included swimming. But I could not swim. Nevertheless, I jumped into the water in the swimming pool and — swam! In the mornings I went to sports college, gave private tuition in the afternoon, and pursued my own sport in the evening. I travelled a lot with the team. I loved the subject of anatomy during this time. I had, in the meantime, become 21 years old.

My life was very hectic from 21 to 27. I travelled and toured with the basketball team. I also taught sport to women and sick children. I freed myself financially from my parents. I attended many holiday courses. When I was 17 I fell in love with a girl while I was teaching sport at a holiday camp. But I soon forgot the matter. I passed my diploma at sports college at 24. After that I taught basketball at technical college. I always stood up for justice there. Later I was also to work as a basketball teacher at university, but I turned down the post.

After that I left all my friends behind and also gave up basketball. I moved back to another town in the interior of the country where I had developed many friendships with farmers. I learned to ride and began to smoke. I was invited to another holiday camp and fell in love with a minister. At 27 I returned to my home town. At this point I broke two ribs while riding. I continued to teach sport in my home town and fell in love with a female pupil. Everyone distanced themselves from me and described me as a lesbian. The whole town talked about me and I lost 20 kg of weight in a short period of time. I did not go to anyone for advice.

I felt great pain when I broke my ribs and one day I felt removed from my body. I had a vision of an old man with a beard and a nurse with instruments, like at an operation, and they healed me. Some time later I was gripped by deep despair; I wanted to kill myself or others. Here too the old man with the beard reappeared and urged me to stay calm, to love and to forgive. During this time I had a vision of a hand with a rose. A being also spoke to me and said that the rebellion of

the others towards me was the result of earlier incarnations
(see Figure 5).

At this point I began a relationship with a girl which lasted
seven years. I often visited the girl in São Paolo.

At 31 I came across the book Occult Science. I read it with
great interest. I had to look after a disabled child to whom I
was deeply attached. I had come to this task through a holiday camp, where disabled children were also accommodated.
I received an offer to go to a Camphill home for a year. I
accepted. After my return I worked mainly with children and
adults in the field of gymnastics. The relationship with my
girlfriend continued.

At 33 I had the inner experience of another being. It said
within me: 'I am the one who was in your mother's tummy.
I have come to help you.' That being accompanied me for a
whole year until I was 34. Then it said: 'This period is finished. You will find your own way now.' At 34 I had a slipped
disc. The doctor wanted to operate but I refused and cured
myself through gymnastics.

Between 34 and 35 I went to the Waldorf school in São
Paolo. I taught there for three and a half years. At 35 I also
started receiving anthroposophical medical treatment at the
Tobias clinic. Shortly afterwards I underwent a haemorrhoid
operation. A friendship started with a girl which lasted four
years. This girl then went to Germany. She was a very important person in my life; she was honest and very courageous.

At 36 I founded my own holiday camp which lay outside
São Paolo. There I did a lot of physical work, and occupied
myself with the horses, plants and trees. I spent every weekend
there in this way. I continued teaching at the São Paolo Waldorf school during the week. I was still working as a gymnastics teacher. I also started an anthroposophical study group.
Then I fell out with the teachers at the Waldorf school and left
the school. I taught mornings and afternoon in a state school.

At 37 another voice came to me which told me: 'You can go
three ways. Don't let your feelings decide. Make sure that you

Figure 5.

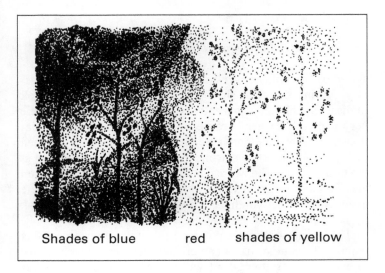

Shades of blue   red   shades of yellow

Figure 6.

open the correct door so that life has meaning!' I was going through a difficult period at the time. When I was 30 I enrolled on a psychomotor studies course which had been set up at the university. I also worked with music a lot during this time. I lost my girlfriend at the age of 39-40 because, as I said, she went to Germany.

I entered a deep crisis in my mid forties. I left the holiday camp, locked my house and was incapable of work for a year. I noticed that I drove out of the city in my car on a number of occasions and left the city behind me. I experienced life as having no meaning and felt listless. At the same time I was very restless. There was a great contradiction between feeling and thinking within me. I went to my doctor again but asked him not to admit me to hospital. This crisis lasted six weeks and I came to terms with it myself. I sometimes drove to the holiday camp on my own during this year. At 42 I noticed how my head was beginning to control and order things again. I started work again. I had to force myself to do so at the beginning. Neither was it easy to find a teaching post since there were many political currents at the university at that time. The drawing 'The Split' (Figure 6) originates at that time.

We know a further seven-year-period in this woman's lifestory. During this time she opened a holiday camp and took in disabled children. This activity lasted two years; they were very difficult for her because of problems in personal relationships. When a curative education day school was opened in São Paolo she started work there. She was 46 years old at the time. Today she works mainly with paralysed children and does movement exercises with them. The old 'muscle experience' of her youth has been transformed into a new task in life.

The strong will element can be felt in the lifestory of this woman. The author has a choleric temperament which comes to expression as strength of will but which also plunges her into conflict. Her homosexuality also leads to many difficult situations for her. She has various supersensory threshold experiences during her life which lead her to the edge of a psychiatric disorder at the age of 42. But she finds her own way out of that crisis. Externally, she has to struggle with work difficulties but they do guide her to her actual life impulse: the work with paralysed children. The experience of her own muscles is transformed into work with paralysed children. We can clearly recognize the mirror images in her lifestory here. In a later chapter of this book we will deal with the way in which the phase from 14 to 21 is reflected in the age from 42 to 49 (see below, p.143).

4. The fulfilment of the human being — spiritual development: from 42 to 63

We now turn to the major phase of spiritual development which occurs in the period from 42 to 63. Many people believe that they have to light a great spiritual sun during this time. But in our experience it is better to ignite just a small light such as a candle and ensure that it does not go out. A single candle or even a match are sufficient to illuminate a dark room. If we demand too much, we run the risk of failing thoroughly. To use another image: those who climb too high during this phase have all the deeper to fall.

The phase between 42 and 63 may be described as the 'phase of human fulfilment.' The fruits of our life ripen during these three seven-year-periods. We would like to give away those fruits, of course, because we ourselves might consume only four or five fruits from the whole tree. But how do we do that? Should we give them to people who are not hungry? Or do we let them rot? No, we have to awaken an interest in the fruits; they might have ripened particularly well for instance. And then, if we manage to make them really attractive to others everyone will want one and they will be eaten with pleasure.

We can place the forces which have in part separated from our organs in the service of our consciousness. They turn into new spiritual organs of perception. If we succeed in doing this we are well on the way to wisdom. We will see in what follows, how in the course of the next three seven-year-periods these forces separate from the three organic systems — the nervous and sensory system, the rhythmical system (heart and lungs) and the metabolic and limb system — and can be metamorphosed into new abilities. We have mostly achieved our personal objectives in this phase and are increasingly able to serve the objectives of humankind — if we pay attention to the inner questions and necessities.

The fairy tale of 'Mother Holle' (or 'Old Mother Frost' as the story is also known) can give us a hint regarding this stage of life: The step daughter has worked all her life, she spins her fingers raw and she jumps into the well in pursuit of her spindle. She comes to the meadow and listens to the questions which come towards her: The bread has been baked and wants to be taken out of the oven. The ripe apples want to be picked up, and Mother Holle's feather beds must be shaken. The longing for the earth drives the step daughter to go home. There she is rewarded and turns into Goldmarie, the golden maiden. Her being can shine in light and wisdom. The lazy daughter, on the other hand, jumps into the well without indulging in any effort or hard work. She can hear the questions perfectly well but she does not do her work, or only in a slovenly way. She wants to reap her reward quickly. But she is rewarded with a shower of pitch.

Our body will be affected if we do not use the forces which are released from our organs. Illnesses appear, particularly growths (including cancer). Or our soul cannot realize its potential in the light and becomes dark. That may lead to depressive states. This is a kind of 'Pitchmarie,' the dirty maiden, effect.

From 42 to 49: New creativity

Everyone knows the expression 'life begins at 40.' But what is it exactly that starts at 40? At 40 our 'I,' which has been tied to the organs, begins gradually to separate from the lower organs. That applies both to the reproductive organs, and the limbs and metabolic system. We can no longer manage to digest a huge steak as we did in earlier years. It weighs on our stomach — a sign that the juices in our digestive system are becoming less.

Men, above all, frequently complain of their muscles no longer being so strong and that their legs are becoming thinner. The desire arises in many at this point to do fitness training in order to counter the fading of the muscles. At the same time this is a phase of increased sexuality since we become especially aware of the organs from which these forces are withdrawing. Women often suffer from abdominal disorders such a myomas or even abdominal carcinoma in the genital area. The forces from these organs and from our muscles are the same which are now used in transformed form for a new creativity. 'Life begins at forty': That means developing new creativity which each person has to find in his or her own way. For many people this means developing a new creativity in their work.

The question which we must pose ourselves during this time is approximately the following: What might we have buried by way of gifts, talents, etc., which we now want to resurrect and allow to develop a new creativity? Or we might ask ourselves: What new impulses are arising within us? We live in a phase in which we can still be quite active and develop many new initiatives. Perhaps we turn our life experience into teaching activity for others.

Men frequently fear losing their position at work and in society, their status. That can lead to longer hours spent at work and less leisure time. It can also be experienced frequently how men prevent the passing on of knowledge and information to younger people at work instead of adopting an altruistic attitude. By this means they keep control of power and status. And those men who failed to develop their feeling side, their female side (the 'anima'), now tend towards excesses. They are constantly searching for new affairs in order to replace from outside what they have failed to develop from inside.

Many divorces take place during this time after the age of 40 — partly for the above reasons, partly because men succumb to the illusion of increased sexuality which comes from the sexual organs. Not for nothing do we have the humorous saying: 'A man swaps his forty-year-old wife for two twenty-year-olds — but can't satisfy either of them.'

What happens with women? They often throw themselves into busy activity by looking after the children or grandchildren. By this means they seek to escape the emptiness in the house which the children may already have left. But many women use this time and the resultant leisure finally to do something for themselves. We can see that very nicely with the woman in Lifestory 7 (p.113).

Women who are deeply involved in jobs face the same problems as men. They too can develop into a wise boss or secretary, or they may become the frustrated, ghastly and impossible person of whom people say: 'I hope that she soon gets over the change in life.' Women who were suppressed by their husbands for years and burdened by the household and children can develop undreamt of activity in the seventh seven-year-period and display their repressed male soul, the 'animus.' Here, too, of course it matters what form this takes. Women can over-emphasize their male soul, or allow their liberated potential to turn into meaningful activity.

There is an additional factor for many women, which is that they become concerned about their physical looks and attractiveness. Some women use medical treatments to try and have more children, but perhaps it is also valuable to develop an awareness that the time has come to bear 'spiritual children.' Women, too, must ask themselves in what field they can develop new creativity.

In the last chapter we compared our situation around the age of 42 with climbing a mountain. When we have reached the summit we see a panoramic view of the landscape lying below us. We can reorientate ourselves and recognize the order, the structure of the landscape. The same can happen after 42 with the 'landscape' of our life. We can therefore describe the stage of life which we now enter as a 'new vision.' We approach a new learning process: We have to learn to look at our life from a higher vantage point while at the same time rapidly grasping the phenomena of external life, the situations and their requirements.

But here lies a further difficulty. On the one hand we want to communicate what we have seen to others. On the other hand we are dealing with a generation which may be somewhere between 21 and 28 and which actually wants to learn by its own experience. We do after all make many mistakes precisely between the ages of 21 and 28 from which we gather our life experience. The older person has an overview of a given situation but there is little sense in telling a younger person: 'Don't you see the consequences of what you are doing?'

Thus we face the question: How can we communicate what we see to younger people? On the one hand we want to give, and on the other we have to restrain ourselves and wait until the younger people come and ask us. The phase in which we develop wisdom begins after the age of 42. Wisdom also means holding back until asked. We can act like a guardian angel for younger people, only intervening at the point where we see that mistakes could lead to accidents. We have to develop a new leadership style if we want to help young people. We can help them a great deal, for example, by assessing their work from time to time. It is important for them regularly to see the results of their work. This strengthens their 'I.' It is therefore also important that their work is acknowledged and assessed in a healthy way, and that the younger people achieve greater objectivity. A good superior at work, for instance, can become a godsend for the younger generation.

But a new leadership style also means passing on increasing numbers of tasks to younger people, which in this context means those between 35 and 42 who have some professional experience. And we have to introduce other people into our own area of work and train them to do it. If we have founded a business and do not at this point ensure a successor we can be sure that the business will go under.

A 48-year-old man who attended one of our lifestory courses realized that he had not done anything about finding a successor for his business. He owned a company with more than four hundred staff. He was still at the centre and controlled everything. During the lifestory course — when he was describing this section of his life — he became aware of the condition his business was in. He then tried to find a quick solution. He wanted to fetch his 20-year-old daughter, who had just started studying architecture, into the company. A younger sister, who was already working in the company as secretary, was to be given responsible duties. A short time afterwards this sister herself visited our lifestory course from a feeling of desperation at having to take on too much responsibility. That is not, of course, the way to resolve such a situation. Care has to be taken that staff at a mature age, perhaps in their mid thirties, are prepared for and introduced to the succession. It is not enough to be a family member, one has to know, above all, what one is doing.

In such a situation, too, then it is a matter of finding the golden mean. If people hand over their duties to others too early they often begin to experience emptiness and do not quite know what they should do with their lives. And if they continue to work to an advanced age and have no time for hobbies, they do not know what to do with their leisure time later. The right measure must be found, but each person has a slightly different measure.

Another course participant, who was in his early fifties, had passed on his duties well and in good time so that there was practically nothing left for him to do except go into the office once a week. He now had to fight against the emptiness which had entered his life. Well, the opportunity came to help his son-in-law build up a farm. He also built up his own farm and in doing so was able to realize both his hobby and his life-long dream.

But if one is already in one's early sixties, manages a large business with 3000 employees, and has failed to train junior staff in good time one is faced with a real problem. The only solution in such a situation is to make use of a consultant who

runs training programmes for junior staff. After all, one's own
children generally want to do something completely different.
The urge to follow one's own individual path is increasingly
strong and young people, if they do not have a particular gift in
this direction, are less than keen to take over the family business, transform it and develop it further.

From 49 to 56: A new way of listening

The phase from 49 to 56 is a time in which forces withdraw
from the rhythmical system of the middle, the lungs and the
heart. Now it is particularly important to find a new rhythm.
These organs will be damaged if we do not succeed in making such a change and continue at our former pace. The result
is a heart attack or problems with the respiratory organs. We
failed to take any breaks to look back on our life and have
now been forced to come to a halt in a way which we did not
really want.

Bernard Lievegoed describes this time as the 'moral phase.'
We might also call it the 'moral and ethical phase.' We quote
a small example to illustrate the heart as organ of conscience
or morality: There are innumerable child-beggars in developing countries who rush towards you and assail you. You have
a principle: I will not give them any money because they will
only use it for drugs or something similar. You therefore say a
decisive no and continue on your way. They look at you with
eloquent eyes, you turn around once more and their eyes meet
yours. Suddenly you do not 'have the heart' to walk on and
you give them some money after all. Your heart has spoken
and overruled your head.

What opportunities arise at this stage for a better understanding of the world? Can we develop new organs of perception? Increasingly during this phase we no longer concern
ourselves exclusively with our individual destiny but with the
destiny of humankind as a whole. The organ of kindness — the

heart — awakens and leads us to suffer and feel sympathy with the whole of humankind.

Let us illustrate this again with a concrete real example: A young man who married at 20 belongs to the staff of a company manufacturing artificial fertilizers and agro-chemicals. He wants to start a family, build a house, own a car. At 30 he heads a whole department, including some sales staff, and he is concerned for the welfare of his subordinates, whether they are also getting their home, their car and their other entitlements. This man begins to acquire a knowledge of ecology in his mid-fifties and is shocked at the ruthless way in which herbicides and artificial fertilizers are used in Brazil. He becomes increasingly concerned about the matter. He no longer feels comfortable selling such products. He has also bought a farm in recent years which he tries to farm organically. How, then, does he adjust? After all, he can hardly just throw his job out of the window and start something new. So what does he do? He looks for organic products and natural fertilizers and begins to sell them along with the other products. Gradually this activity becomes the most important one. The man's objective in the long run is to stop selling products using artificial fertilizers altogether. His conscience has made its voice heard; it is important to listen to the voice of the heart and not to allow it to be drowned out by the lust for power. This examples demonstrated the gradual transition from one activity to another.

It is important that we should adopt a beneficent stance during this phase of our life. Or to put it another way, we become a 'universal father' or 'universal mother.' Our children have grown up and have mostly left home. We can frequently observe how our own children hardly ask us for advice but that the friends of our children do so all the more. We experience our existence as father and mother being extended to a whole generation of young people. In such circumstances our house may become a home in which young people come and go in a happy and relaxed atmosphere.

Now is also the most appropriate age at which to turn to politics in the best sense of the word in order to attempt to do something for people, country and humankind in this field.

The phase from the early to the mid fifties is a harmonious time which ends in a rather more difficult transition. For not only do human beings enter a new stage of life, but 56 is also the time of the third lunar node. What may happen in this phase? We can illustrate this, too, with a concrete example. A man in his mid-fifties worked all his life in a multinational company and founded many branches throughout Brazil. His intensive work meant that he devoted too little time to his wife and five children. In his early fifties he began to notice how he was becoming more and more lonely. His wife and children no longer understood him and he did not understand them any more. This made him aware of the extent to which he had neglected his family. He wanted to make up what he had omitted to do thus far. That was hardly possible, of course. He built a big house on the beach in the shape of a five-pointed star and furnished a flat for each of the children. The middle of the house was to be a large communal room. But the man was faced with the bitter experience that his children never entered the house. In the end he was left with no other option than to make the house available for Christmas holidays and charitable purposes. He himself left the firm but he did not succeed in making a healthy transition. He continued to suffer from too high blood pressure and heart problems. The man then decided to go to the Amazon basin and start new cocoa and other plantations. In other words, he devoted himself to new pioneering tasks. Unfortunately we have not heard from him since. But we know that his heart and circulatory problems have worsened. The relationship with his family has not improved either.

Let us now look at the lifestory of a woman of 62:

Lifestory 7

A course participant of the age of 62 reports that she was always regarded as the ugly duckling by her parents. Her siblings were always the favourites. She began working at the age of 14 and had to earn her own keep although she still lived in her parents' home. She married a doctor at 21. She had no inclination to study although her husband encouraged her to do so. She had two children in her fourth seven-year-period. As well as bringing up the children, she ran a record and tape shop in order to contribute something to the family income. Her husband fell ill with a manic depressive psychosis when she reached the age of 40. A short while later she herself fell ill with thyroid cancer. Death was staring her in the face. But she slowly began to recover after X-ray treatment. At the age of 42 she began to study art at university. She organized exhibitions, was successful and won prizes. Her husband, however, was unable to cope with her success and so she gave up this activity again for quite some time. She then began to make weaving looms and to teach the simple country women how to weave. She designed patterns for the women to weave and started a real small textile industry in three different places in the interior of the state of Minas Gerais. She passed the orders for woven rugs on to the women and collected the finished rugs for sale.

But she was not spared hard blows of fate. Her son had become a drug addict at the age of 13. At 20 he was involved in a serious car accident, as the result of which he was temporarily paralysed and required her help for more than two years until he regained his movement. He then lived with a woman who was also a drug addict; they had children and finally married. He experienced a psychomanic-depressive episode on three occasions and three times he tried to commit suicide. On each occasion it was his mother who was the only one to stand by him and help him over the crisis. The daughter

*of the woman also become involved with a drug user at an
early age. She had two children which she wanted to leave
with her mother so that she could pursue her work.*

*Thus our patient kept being involved in the destiny of others
and had great difficulty in pursuing her own work. She became
ill with cancer of the bladder when she had just turned 62.
She has now recovered from that and has entered a phase of
her existence in which she finally wants to pursue her own life
together with her 67-year-old husband. But in all the preceding years she was able to develop her creativity with the rug
factory. During this time her husband suffered another manic-
depressive episode during which he donated the whole of his
practice to a young female colleague. He did not, then, make
things easy for his wife.*

*Our patient possesses extraordinary courage with which to
face life. She believes that she is able, finally, to become less
aggressive and spend the remaining years of her life in greater
peace. She was brought up in a Protestant household and keeps
to the text of the Bible. Beyond that, she is progressing towards
an understanding of a more comprehensive spiritual dimension.*

This lifestory demonstrates clearly those elements which, on
the one hand, are part of the general development and the
crises faced by each person in the various phases of his or
her life and those elements which, on the other hand, possess a more individual character and constitutes a person's
individual destiny. The seven-year-periods of this women
are strongly delineated. She begins work at 14, marries at 21,
and between the ages of 21 and 28 she has her two children.
Then the externals blows of fate occur such as her husband's
illness. This has such a dramatic effect on her that it probably triggers the thyroid carcinoma in her. She comes close
to death. At 42, once again at the start of a new seven-year-
period, the elements of resurrection come into play. New
values arise and she decides to study. But although she is
successful, she allows herself to be suppressed once again.

Then she manages to combine her creativity with work and in the phase from 42 to 49 she develops quite new activities. Although blows of fate continue to rain down on her she carries on with her newly found activities throughout the period from 49 to 56 and into her sixty-third year. The seeds which were planted inside her from the age of 42 onwards were able to blossom despite the difficult external circumstances.

In my own lifestory I began to develop a greater interest in the psychological aspects of the human being from the age of 42 onwards. I have also conquered the fear of encountering psychiatric patients which I have had since childhood. In my mid forties, large numbers of young doctors and medical students who wanted to acquire a knowledge of anthroposophical medicine came to my colleagues and me. Although I had never before in my life thought of teaching, we were forced to confront this question by outside developments and began to organize medical seminars with the help of a number of external lecturers. Furthermore, there were growing numbers of young doctors who wanted to work for a year in the clinic as junior doctors. In this way my purely medical activity on behalf of the patients was transformed into teaching activity. There were other new elements: Acquiring a knowledge of social education and skills for leading group activities, as well as a deeper interest in the developmental possibilities of each person through lifestory work. This new activity was subsequently given a new framework: 'Artemisia' was founded and inaugurated in my fifty-second year — the centre at which our lifestory seminars are held. Since then my work has been concentrated increasingly in this field.

Goethe intensively studied the laws of plant metamorphosis. His discoveries have helped us to observe plants more attentively and to understand them better. Their development is not an abrupt but a continuous one. It would not make sense to imagine that plants have to destroy themselves in order to produce blossoms and fruits. On the contrary, we are looking

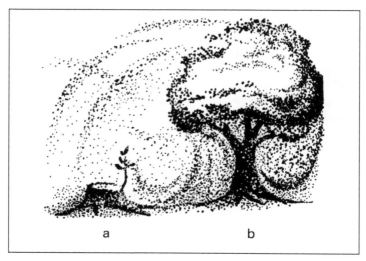

Figure 7.

at a natural, organic process. The same applies to our own lifestory. Here too we discover, if we look more closely, a process of metamorphosis, of transformation. And this process of gradual transformation is very important. It is therefore essential that we work to transform our abilities and do not throw everything which we have learnt and done away, as it were, in order to start something new. We always build on steps which we have constructed ourselves and we have to use these steps to continue on upwards.

Wisdom can truly blossom in the period from 49 to 56. We might also call this period the phase of inspirational soul development. It is particularly important to learn to listen to what is going on around us. What questions does the external environment pose? Some people do not know in this phase of their life what they should do. The children have left home in the case of many women and they are looking for new activities. But there is little merit in trying to impose our activities and our impulses on the world. It does make sense, however, for us to learn to listen to an ever greater degree. Inspiration is connected with breathing in. We breathe in what the world is telling us — or what our inner voice reveals to us. Listening in this way has a dual aspect, turning towards the outside and the inside. The forces which separate themselves from the body during this phase, particularly from the respiratory system, enable us increasingly to use this new organ of perception which is linked to listening. We achieve ever greater harmony with the cosmos and in particular those rhythms of the cosmos which are reflected in the heart and lungs. Think of Beethoven, who was almost deaf in the final years of his life but who increasingly heard his inner music — the music of the spheres.

The following exercise can help us a great deal during this time as well as in the following two phases of our life. That is particularly the case when we are overburdened with duties and work: Imagine your duties and also your human relationships as the branches of a tree. Then look which branches must be sawn off so that there can be new growth. Such an exercise, combined with drawing, produces interesting results, as in the above picture for example.

It was done by a 32-year-old participant at a lifestory course. He has sawn off the whole rotten tree in his picture but has not touched the shoot (a). The exercise then develops further towards asking: What does this tree need so that it can grow to full strength in a new direction? The next step in drawing is to depict the tree as one imagines it in the future (b).

The course participant who drew this picture went through a difficult childhood and youth. He grew up without his father or mother and began working at a very early age. He led a life full of excesses in his twenties. His first marriage lasted from 30 to 36 and he was professionally very successful. He married again at 42 and that is when he started his family. Aged 52 — he has two relatively small children — he is dissatisfied with his material success and his job. But new perspectives are opening up for him — that can be seen from the beautiful tree which has grown from the shoot.

The following poem has the same thrust:

Slowly you feel how your 'I' becomes stronger
How a royal tree unfolds from the thin shoot –
One tree among many –
How well I feel –
How proud and full of success –
Recognized and respected –
I have found my 'I' –
I can stride through life, proud and secure –
Until one day, perhaps a little tired from the long journey,
I sit down under a tree –
But, misery, I no longer see the sky
For all the leaves and branches!
Neither sun, nor clouds nor the blue sky –
Neither moon nor stars nor the dark of night.
Horrified I jump up — where are you?
Shocked I see a long shadow on the ground –
From the moon which throws his pale light on me from
     far away –
That is me?
When I wake up the next morning
My first impulse is –
To use pickaxe, axe and saw
To cut the branches –
Be able to breathe again –
See light, see the blue sky again
and the peaceful shine of the stars! –
No, that is no life –
Where is my partner — where my child?
But the tree, very hurt, speaks:
Can't you wait?
Don't you see the ripening fruits?
Soon autumn will be here — you fool –
The leaves are falling, the fruit is ripening,
And all will sing your praises

in a great 'O' –
Your fruit is sweet –
You can feed many –
People, animals — large and small –
All will be grateful to you –
Do not destroy it — give it away –
Sun and moon will shine through the branches again –
You stand there, deep in thought,
Silver haired.
With eyes shining like the sun –
No matter whether you can see or not.
Of the stars looking through the branches –
One already waves to you in such a homely, friendly
      manner –
I come from in front there –
That is where I am going –
With a profound 'U' I bow to you –
And consciously I see:
That is how I am.

From 56 to 63: The 'intuitive side'

Now let us turn to the phase from 56 to 63. This is a difficult
time of introversion. Bernard Lievegoed calls it the mystical
phase. It is the time in which some people have the opportunity
to turn into spiritual leaders. But here again the fact applies that
such spiritual leaders do not run after others to proclaim their
wisdom but that they wait until people come to them.

It took me a long time to understand why the ninth seven-
year-period is described as the mystical phase. We can also
describe it as the period of the intuitive soul. At this stage we
are in diametrical opposition to the first seven-year-period. In
the first seven years of our life the world was revealed to use
through our senses. We were incarnated through the sensory
world, made contact with the external world through our

senses. Now we have reached the point where our senses, the windows to the outside world, are slowly closing. Our ears no longer hear so well, we need glasses, and our sense of touch is also becoming blunted. Or we complain that the soup no longer tastes the same. But it is the same as always, it is our sense of taste which is no longer as acute. Often we are no longer able to distinguish the scent of flowers or we lose our delicate perception of what is going on in our fellow human beings or what they want to express. These senses, too, must be intensively cultivated so that we can maintain and use them. I refer in this context to the two books by Norbert Glas: *Gefährdung und Heilung der Sinne* and *Fulfillment in Old Age*. We must therefore quite consciously do something for our senses if they are to continue to mediate our contact with the world. It is a fact, on the other hand, that our body increasingly becomes a cave in which we live as hermits and in this sense we are dependent on our spiritual light. We are more strongly in touch with our spiritual side, or the God in us, as some express it — that is why we refer to intuition.

The being of a little child is a shining light in the world. We have the impression that the personality of the child is much larger than its body. In mid-life our spiritual being is immersed in our body. It is eclipsed and we are chained deeply to the earth. But that is precisely why we are able to let the spiritual element which we have brought with us into our incarnation flow deep into the earth. In old age our body becomes increasingly transparent. Our bones become lighter, we suffer from osteoporosis, that is a loss of calcium in the bones, and our being can begin increasingly to shine from the inside to the outside. Why, for instance, do small children love their grandparents so much? Because they can experience this shining light with them. And if the body avoids falling prey to heaviness and continues to be carried lightly, then this light becomes visible. If the light remains invisible, it is as if the sun is hidden behind clouds. This means that our physical body has become so solidified and sclerotic that we can no longer penetrate it.

The light and the sun can then no longer shine through it, like with clouds. It frequently happens that people at this age have a tendency towards premature sclerotization. This means primarily that the blood vessels in the brain harden through premature calcification. That manifests itself in inflexibility in the thinking, forgetfulness and pig-headedness. If the life forces have been insufficiently cared for and respected in the first seven-year-period — by, for example, starting school too early or making too many demands of the intellect — then the brain loses its vitality too early and the predisposition for premature sclerosis is given. It frequently happens that the consequences arising from early childhood only become evident at this stage, in the phase from 56 to 63. There are, of course, always opportunities in life to take preventive therapeutic action. Every artistic therapy, every exercise of the thinking, every creative act as such strengthens the human being in this sense.

The ninth seven-year-period is a time in which we often have to cope with illness as well. We have to learn to deal with it for the rest of our lives. We might suffer from diabetes, or back ache or too high blood pressure. Often these manifestations force us to change our lifestyle or our nutrition. We have to learn renunciation at this stage and such illnesses are sometimes a help in this respect.

Often we enter retirement in these years and should have learnt to pursue a hobby. We might have been looking forward to such an activity for a long time and have already made arrangements with this in mind. But anyone who does not prepare for these years will experience emptiness. There are many jobs in which the step to retirement does not play such a decisive role. A doctor, or an artist or a lawyer might develop their abilities to the full only at this stage. Many other people, in contrast, who were active in a technological job in which it was hardly possible to keep up any longer with the latest developments, are confronted with inner emptiness at this stage. They then have to fill this emptiness with something. Not to do so leads to depression or alcoholism.

We live in a phase in which we like to look back on our
life. Many people write their lifestory. We often observe in
our lifestory course how people who come to us after the age
of 63 have lost interest in their own lifestory. They cannot
muster the strength or the courage to look at their lives with
sufficient clarity. That is why in the ninth seven-year-period
— and of course the preceding years — it is very important
to look back on our lives, on what we have achieved, what
abilities we have developed and what we want to carry forward into the future. These are all questions which require
answers and which help us to move forward in our life in a
meaningful way.

In my own lifestory — when I was 56 years old — I felt: If
I do not develop a new impulse at this stage in my life I will
wither and shrivel up in my soul and spirit, and my physical
decline will be accompanied by soul and spiritual decline.
Thereafter it took about two years before it became clear what
my task in this seven-year-period would be. Our life begins
to develop steadily again from the moment that we find the
thread once more.

The author of Lifestory 1 (p.24) made the following com-
ment on this phase: 'My life has become my philosophy of
life.' After all, each person has led an extraordinarily rich
life and if we work consciously on turning these experiences
into a philosophy of life we will have grasped the task of this
seven-year-period.

This is also a time when material values are no longer of
such importance to us. Often we make our will and divide
up our possessions. But we must be careful to keep enough
to ensure a secure old age for ourselves. Because otherwise
the following years could become very difficult if we have to
continue fighting for our upkeep — as is frequently the case in
Brazil nowadays. Some people require more help in this phase
than is often thought. It is self-evident that our children should
help us when we have grown old. But at this stage they are still
very much concerned with building their own life and have lit-

tle time for the older generation. That is why special attention needs to be paid to people at this stage in life.

When the menopause occurs in women after the age of 49 and the andropause in men after the age of 56, the psychological difference between men and women is reduced somewhat. Forty-nine is the time of the menopause for women. It signifies a change which goes deep into the organic level and triggers a crisis in some women: Now the time when she could have had children is over for good. Since the female hormones are gradually reduced, the number of male hormones increases, relatively speaking. The result on a biological level is a deeper voice and increased hair growth. But there are also changes on a soul level. After a shortish phase of emotional instability, women experience a kind of liberation. They like to adopt 'male' characteristics to a greater extent, become more active and finally feel able to pursue their own instincts and an impulse to become involved in outside activities, which led them into the world. That can frequently be observed in older women.

The so-called andropause occurs somewhat later in men. At around the age of 56 they experience major changes. These do not, however, affect men physically as profoundly as is the case with women. After all, men can still father children at the age of 70 and beyond. Thus all the changes take place to a greater extent on a soul level. Men do not want to lose their male qualities, they frequently want to demonstrate that they are still the same as before. Often the organs cause sexual dreams as they release their forces. If men know that these originate on an organic level they can cope with them better and will not fall prey to the illusion that they need to find themselves a girlfriend. On a soul level the increased number of female hormones can manifest itself in men becoming more domestic.

If a couple has developed sufficient understanding one for the other, the husband will help his wife to overcome the menopause and, conversely, the wife will later help her husband over the andropause. This requires that an intimacy exists between the two which enables them to discuss any problems. Their relationship must develop in a new direction. Their children — if they had any — have probably left home and the couple are alone once more. Can this lead to a new deepening of their relationship? Or do the difficulties and the mutual grumbling increase? Their individual peculiarities are more strongly expressed. Much unnecessary pain and injury to feelings can sometimes be avoided if the couple respects the particular nature of the other.

Lifestory 8: A life told as a fairy tale

In our lifestory courses, we often set the participants the following task: Try to put your lifestory in the form of a fairy tale.

This is one way of distancing oneself from the psychological complications which sometimes set in when one looks back over the course of one's life. By telling one's life in the form of a fairy tale it is easier to distance oneself from it and to gain an overview over the whole of one's lifestory through images.

Below, let us look at the lifestory of a woman who wrote it at the age of 54. The patient was born on 28 October 1930 in the Brazilian state of Minas Gerais. She grew up in a family of many children. She worked as a teacher for some years, then married and stopped work. She devoted herself wholly to her family and made many sacrifices for them. Her husband was the master of the house who determined everything. Later, from about the age of 50 onwards, the woman cultivated a friendship which, however, she kept secret from her family until shortly before her death. The patient died of stomach cancer on 17 December 1991.

The story of a rose bush

Once upon a time there was a beautiful garden. Many flowers lived there in complete harmony: Marguerites, begonias, forget-me-nots, petunias, pansies as well as bushes and foliage plants in many different shapes and colours.

One day towards the end of winter, as all the plants were awakening from their sleep and were preparing to blossom, it happened that a new plant was born. It was a very young rose bush, so young that he himself did not know what a rose looked like. The smaller flowers looked respectfully, tinged with a little fear, up to their new playmate. For apart from his strong stem, the rose bush had prickles! But the latter spoke in such gentle tones that the plants immediately trusted him. Because the garden was so lovely and colourful, the rose bush wanted to show his best side — he made a great effort until he succeeded in producing his first bud from which blossomed a beautiful rose the colour of the sunrise.

One day, as the rose bush was still in the process of drying the last drops of morning dew in the sun, a blue butterfly appeared. 'Oh, what a beautiful, scented rose!' he exclaimed. 'I would love to have a scent like that, but I am no flower, I am a butterfly. But I can fly, can visit other gardens far from here. A rose like you will never be able to see them.'

With these words the butterfly flew away and let his blue wings sway in the breeze. The rose bush looked after him thoughtfully: 'How lovely it would be if I had wings and could also fly. I would be free like the butterfly. But I have such deep roots that they bind me to the earth. Neither wind nor thunderstorms can tear me away from here.' On this day the rose bush was sad because he only had roots instead of wings.

He was still deep in thought when a bee came flying around the roses. 'What a funny animal,' the rose bush thought. 'What do you want from me?' he asked. 'Admire my roses, or breath in my scent?' 'Nothing like that,' answered the bee. 'You should know that I am a busy worker and don't have time for such things. I only want the nectar from inside the blossoms. We bees make honey from that which provides food for the whole hive.' With those words, the bee penetrated the flower, collected the nectar and flew away.

A few days later, a song-thrush came flying through the air and landed next to the rose bush. 'You are enchanting,' she said. 'Always remain as you are and keep a watch on your branches, your roses and your scent. In a word — just be a rose bush!'

'But what about the thorns, which I do not like. And I don't have wings like the butterfly either, only roots which tie me to the ground.'

'The thorns,' the song-thrush said, 'are your weapons against those who would rob your roses. Watch them care-fully, they will serve you well in your hour of need. You do not need to be jealous of the butterflies: They are the messengers of the flowers and that is why they must have wings. And you should be grateful to your roots, for they bring you fresh water from the depths of the earth when the sun is so strong that weaker flowers burn up. Your roots give you strength against the frost, and keep you firm and upright. It is your destiny always to be prepared, firmly at your place like a guard, like a lighthouse.'

'But I want to go away from here, want to get to know the world and become wise.'

'Your wisdom lies here. What do birds know about the secrets of the earth? But you know them. Your roots reach into the depths and collect the liquid which your stem transforms into traces of life, into branches, leaves, thorns and roses. Be nothing but a rose bush and you will be a master!'

Thus the bird spoke and flew away while the rose bush sank into deep thought. Then he heard a loud screech which fright-ened him. It was the sparrow hawk who was calling to him:

'You're dreaming like all rose bushes! Don't take what that bird told you so seriously; he is a merry fellow who only thinks

about his song. Nothing of what he says is important. After all, who can live from roses and scent? The wild mulberry tree gives us much more, for he satisfies our hunger. The leafy bush is also much more useful for he gives us shade on hot days. Beauty and scent — pure vanity! The important thing is to be useful, my son! Always struggle, suffer till the tears come if necessary in order one day to achieve peace. Abandon your present life, don't bother so much with the outer appearance of your roses; learn to serve.'

That night the rose bush had difficulty in sleeping. He kept turning over in his thoughts what he had heard. When morning came, he was really convinced that he was a vain and useless rose bush. He looked about him and saw that he was indeed egotistical, for until then he had not even been aware of the small, delicate plants which came out of the earth around him and had to struggle with their clumsy stems, leaves and blossoms. He decided to become a teacher. Innumerable times he began to teach marguerites, pansies and forget-me-nots how to spread their leaves, form buds and unfold their flowers. He spoke to them of scents and how to spread them gently. He told them about the weeds which were suffocating the small plants and did not let them breathe. He was very sure of himself and thought secretly that this was his own garden of which he was the master. He wanted everything to be well ordered, everything to happen in the right place and time, without disturbing the equilibrium. He felt happy in the knowledge of being wise and just.

But the sparrow-hawk, who was flying nearby, made fun of him and said:

'What comfortable work you have chosen! Advising plants. From the height of your vanity you think that you are king. Being useful, my son, means leaving yourself completely and devoting yourself wholly to others. What do I see when I look at you? The same vain rose bush who is proud of his roses. Look at that beautiful example of self-effacement over there. That bird over there has brought up her young and now she cares

for the cuckoo who has broken out of the abandoned egg.'

And it was true — the mother starling came along followed by her charge, a strong bird who was bigger than her.

'How are you?' asked the rose bush.

'I don't have any time to think about that, for I have much work to do. Life is difficult for someone with responsibilities like me. I am very tired, my feet ache from scratching the ground, my wings are heavy because I have to fly so much, my eyes cannot see well any longer because I have to keep looking for clean water, sweet fruit and a shady tree. I have brought up many children and all of them quickly learnt to fly and look for food; now they live happily in the woods. But this son here creates too much work for me! He is incapable of feeding himself, is always under my feet, screams for food and demands help. That is my fate: old and tired and having to keep on working!'

With these words, mother and son departed.

Time passed and the rose bush felt increasingly unhappy. Each spring the sparrow-hawk appeared to remind him of his duties: 'How are things? Are you still vain and useless?' But everything was bad. It appeared that all the forces of nature wanted the best for him. The roots of the rose bush delved ever deeper into the earth from whence they collected food and guided the juices through their canals into his stem; the stem, which appeared so rigid, processed everything in its innards and nourished and strengthened the branches. Sun and wind made their generous contribution from outside. The shoots sprouted at every opportunity and turned into buds from which the roses blossomed. That was his undoing! Much as he tried, he could not prevent them blossoming. At this time he noticed another plant next to him which was so delicate that its leaves seemed like toys. It began quietly to right itself and twine itself around the nearest stem until it reached the stem of the rose bush. There the creeper found a firm hold and rapidly grew upwards, twined itself around the branches as much as it could, extended new tendrils and continued to strive upwards. At the beginning the rose bush felt uncomfortable. It was a strange feeling to be completely wrapped up by the plant which filled all his spaces and continued to assail him.

'You need love and protection,' the creeper said. 'You are so innocent and defenceless. There is so much wickedness around! From now on I will be here to protect you. I will not allow any harm to come to you.'

'The creeper is right,' the rose bush thought. 'The garden is full of dangers.'

One spring — he remembered it very well — he had tried in vain to blossom. Every time that he started to put out a new twig a sparrow came and ate the bud, a precious bud, which had cost so much labour in vain. Thereafter the wasps came who ate all the buds which were still closed. But now he did not need to fear anything any more. The creeper was there and took care of his twigs; he covered them and protected them from the rigours of the earth. True, he no longer had any roses, but that was not important. During this spring the creeper never stopped blossoming, produced small flowers like stars, and formed a beautiful dense crown which even gave some shade. The rose bush was satisfied in himself. Finally he had become useful. Thanks to him, the creeper was able to grow and was enchanting to look at. All who saw the creeper admired him so much that they no longer remembered that a rose bush had once stood there.

One fine day, a strange bird landed on a branch of the red hibiscus. The rose bush hardly saw him, he had become so covered by the undergrowth of the creeper. But the bird was curious and hoped nearer from one branch to the next until he finally discovered the rose bush. He investigated silently and thoughtfully. Then he asked:

'When will you let your roses bloom? It is spring — it's time for all rose bushes to reveal their colours and scents. You haven't even got a bud yet!'

'None of that is important,' the rose bush said. 'The important thing is to leave oneself behind and give oneself to others. That is the way I have been taught to attain peace. And that is

what I am doing. I am giving my branches to the creeper. Look how he knows how to make himself beautiful! The brilliance of the creeper is my life.'

But the bird replied: *'The important thing is that you should be wholly yourself. Look around you and see how many wretched flowers and bushes there are — but only you are a rose bush. A rose bush who has renounced the task which nature has assigned him. That is why this garden is incomplete. Its harmony must be restored.'*

'What can I do?' the rose bush asked in a quiet voice.

'Fight, reconquer your living space, be confident!'

With that, the little bird flew away. And the rose bush began to meditate. *'How lovely it would be if I could blossom again! That is the only way I could be happy.'* But he lacked the courage to ask the creeper to stop feeding on his strength and to let him live. *'Oh, if only the creeper understood this by himself and would finally decide to leave here!'* Time passed and the opulent and self-confident creeper grew stronger and stronger and wound new branches around the twigs of the rose bush who was quite tired and crushed. *'It is too late to fight,'* he thought. And gradually he lost the will to live. No one heard his sighs of pain, they were so weak.

One summer afternoon, a storm caught a flock of swallows. Since there were no trees in which to seek protection, they sought shelter in the blooming bush of the creeper. They tried to dry their wet feathers as best they could. While they were doing that, they heard the faint lament:

'If only someone could help me!'

The swallows were startled. *'What? A healthy bush like this one asking for help?'* It was only then that they discovered the strong, bent thorns; they belonged to the rose bush.

'What has happened to you? Why are you so sad?' they asked.

'I would like to blossom but no longer have the strength to do so.'

'We will help you,' the swallows said immediately.

'And what will happen to the creeper?'

'He has to learn to use his own strength.'

Then the swallows began in patient work to liberate the branches of the rose bush one by one. The rose bush sighed deeply and fell asleep, for he was very tired.

Once separated from the rose bush, the creeper lamented his fate and tried to separate his tangle of branches.

'Do you want help as well?' the swallows asked.

'No!' was the answer, for the creeper was very proud of his power. And the swallows flew away.

The rosebush slept through the autumn. He dreamt of a new spring full of sun, flowers, butterflies and song-birds. And he saw in his dream how the creeper climbed up poles of expensive wood, stretching out his star-blossom covered branches in all directions. Refreshed, the rose bush opened his eyes to face life. Signs of the ending winter were in the air; it was time to prepare for the blossoms.

Things will be fulfilled and ordered,
But you need to have the patience
So that over years and in the furrows
Happiness is free to grow.

Then one day you'll sense the ripeness
Of the corn and its maturing
And you'll rise to start the harvest
Thus to fill the deepest storehouse.

Christian Morgenstern

5. The last stages in life

From the age of 63 onwards, we begin to free ourselves from the web of destiny. This moment is often experienced as a rebirth. Many minor physical ailments disappear and our general health also improves. The course of our remaining life is still, of course, linked with the preceding periods, mainly from the age of 42 onwards: our development, whether or not we displayed courage and creativity from 42 to 49, whether or not a new rhythm and wisdom were found between 49 and 56, and whether or not we developed inwardness and patience in the last seven-year-period. The seven-year cycles now run into one another, and the breaks become less clear. They are linked to a greater extent to each person's individual destiny.

Old age has become an increasing problem in our society today. The whole of family life has become less secure and the cohesion of the extended family is absent. Certainly, there are old people's homes, but it is exceedingly important that they should be places where the possibility of spiritual development exists and not places where the elderly simply criticize one another and grumble about their ailments.

Our physical forces continue to decline and the spiritual and soul part of us continues the process of separation from the body. That enables us, on the one hand, to overcome our physical ailments. We feel liberated and in a position to turn our attention to a cosmic existence. This enables our consciousness to expand indefinitely and we achieve new insights. On the other hand we are now able to develop greater modesty and selflessness. Furthermore, we are able to turn our attention in increasing measure to charitable and social tasks. Everyone has to find their own field of endeavour of course. Some charitable work takes so much effort that the person no longer has sufficient time to undertake spiritual and creative work.

Many people start an artistic activity at this time, painting for example. In the US there is a painting school in the Grand Canyon which older people can attend from the age of 70 onwards. And such organizations which promote the artistic element in the elderly exist all over the world.

We may continue to divide the course of a person's life into seven-year-cycles. The next three seven-year-periods have one characteristic in common. During this time the older person can practise qualities which were decisive for the initial seven-year-periods.

From 63 to 70 we allow the quality of wonder to arise in us again: a new attitude of wonder towards nature, our surroundings, our grandchildren who are developing into ever stronger personalities. If we look back to childhood again during this period, we develop a feeling of gratitude. We can allow that child to arise in us once more. Patience and self-training help us overcome serious obstacles; we radiate true benevolence. Often we meet elderly people who give a markedly youthful impression — not so much in the way they look as in their behaviour.

The period from 70 to 77

Let us look back to our second seven-year-period once more. The qualities which we acquired during that time through education now come into their own. There is a saying that a person who bent his knee in prayer as a child gets strong legs. And this influence of childhood is particularly noticeable in old age. In her book *Cosmic Citizen*, Beredene Jocelyn makes the point that anyone who looked up in reverence to someone as a child and folded their hands in prayer will have the capacity to bless in old age. The beauty of the world is also experienced in quite a new way now.

The average human lifespan is approximately 72 years.

That is connected with the rhythm of the sun; in its exact motion it moves by one degree within a period of 72 years which means that our birth star is no longer fully aligned with the sun. Rudolf Steiner says in one of his karma lectures that a person's birth star begins to work against him when that occurs. If we still live on earth after this period it is a true blessing. Our pulse rate too, incidentally, represents a sun rhythm with an approximate 72 beats per minute.

The elderly person now has a true capacity to radiate peace, act as a blessing to others and extend sympathy. One patient said at this age: 'I fly like an eagle over the landscape and settle where I am needed.' (She had five children and many grandchildren.) Such an attitude is more productive than feeling slighted because one is lonely or has not been given enough attention.

The phase from 77 to 84

In this phase the youth in us emerges again. We are engaged in a renewed striving for truth. Death is approaching and we should make an effort to let our bad habits die. We have to face ourselves in truth and justice, clear our conscience and make our peace with other people.

We may experience these three stages, the three seven-year-periods, like a mountain landscape. We see a ridge before us and walk towards it. When we have climbed it we discover another one behind it. And beyond that one another summit becomes visible. Thus we stride with strength and courage into ever further dimensions.

Each person's lifespan is of course quite different. It depends on individual destiny. One might have had a short life and yet have exerted an exceedingly important influence on the world — like Mozart for instance or other great geniuses. Alternatively, one might live a long time and leave nothing behind. It is particularly important for a fruitful life that we are always prepared to learn something new for as long as we live. All aspects of life, however negative they may seem, present valuable learning experiences by which people can acquire new abilities.

Completely new opportunities in life are also seen by people who already arrived at the threshold of death and who at that moment saw their life flash past them like a film. Their lifestory is given a quite new direction once they return to life.

We look back on our life and try to recognize the positive points in our lifestory which always served to refresh our courage to live. What might we have done better? Where did the friction occur which caused difficulties in our inter-personal relations? Is there still an opportunity during our remaining lifetime to rectify that? If we throw a greater light on the course of our life through such work on our own lifestory, we are less burdened when we pass through the portal of death and are able to work on our destiny with greater consciousness.

Steps

As every flower dies and all youth
Gives way to old age, so blossoms every stage of life,
Blossoms all wisdom and every virtue
In its time and cannot last for ever.
The heart must be prepared to say goodbye
And make a new start when life calls,
To enter new commitments
With courage and no sadness.
And every start contains an element of magic
Which protects us and helps us live.

Cheerfully we should stride from room to room
And cling to none as if it were our home.
The spirit of the world does not desire to tie us
    and restrict us,
But, step by step, to raise and broaden us.
No sooner do we feel at home in our surroundings
And snugly settled in, we slacken.
Even at the hour of death we might
Be sent youthfully to new realms,
And never will the call of life come to an end ...
Well then, my heart, take leave and heal thyself!

Hermann Hesse

6. Rhythms and mirror images of life development

If we look at the sea, we observe a wave gradually approaching. It continues to grow until it finally breaks. There is a great whirlpool and then the water runs on. The same is true of our life. Here, too, there are phases when a development continues to escalate, we experience climaxes and situations of change, followed by longer phases of development. We will pursue the various phases and rhythms in a person's lifestory a little in this chapter. We will do this with reference to our reflections in previous chapters and will provide an overview of important developments.

We mostly celebrate our tenth, twentieth, thirtieth, fiftieth birthday and so on in a special way. Many couples celebrate their silver wedding after 25 years, and their golden wedding after 50 years. These are periods which we find particularly impressive on an outward level. These are round figures and we might have the feeling that certain phases of our life have been rounded off.

But we can also subdivide the three great phases of life as we described them in our general overview — the phases of physical, soul and spiritual development — into three smaller ones with the result that there are seven years to each division. This rhythm presents us with major changes which sometimes go as far as creating a crisis in our life. We might say that every seven years we reach a higher stage in our life — or, in the words of a popular saying, every seven years we change our skin. That means that our inside no longer quite fits our outside and the latter must be rejected, as it were, or transformed.

The seven year rhythm has its origin in cosmic laws. Like the weekly rhythm (the seven-day rhythm) it has its own dynamic. Everyone knows that a Saturday is different from a Monday: the start of the week has a different character to the end of the week. In some languages these days are associated with various planets: *Saturday* with Saturn, *Sunday* with the Sun, *Monday* with the Moon; in French we find the link between *mardi* and Mars, *mercredi* and Mercury, *jeudi* and Jupiter, *vendredi* and Venus. The planetary forces affect human existence They particularly act on the various seven-year-periods in a person's life. They form and renew forces in the human being during the night, when the soul and spiritual element separates from the physical and biological elements in order to penetrate higher spheres — a similar process to the one which takes place between death and a new birth. As spiritual beings we dwell in the various 'chambers of God' in order to assimilate special forces connected with our destiny.

Thus from conception to birth we are exposed to Moon forces which play a key role in determining our form and constitution. From seven to 14, school age, the forces of Mercury are active with their health-giving and harmonizing influence. From puberty onwards it is mainly the forces of Venus at work; they exercise an intensive influence on the erotic sphere and the ideas and ideals of the third seven-year-period. From 21 to 42 we come under the influence of the sun sphere, which particularly forms our soul development. This sphere is the dwelling place where the spiritual core of the human being (the spiritual individual or, as Goethe described it, the eternal entelechy) spends most of its life after death. That is why it also spans the longest period in the human lifestory. This is the sphere from which human beings draw the power to assimilate past events (up to the age of 21) and develop them onwards. From this period onwards we have the opportunity increasingly to stride into the future and liberate ourselves from the past in order to realize the aims we have set ourselves in life. From 49 to 56 the Jupiter forces are particularly active. They enable us to structure the course of our life with increasing wisdom. Finally, the forces of Saturn are active from 56 to 63; they allow us to look back on our life, which enables us to adopt a questioning attitude: Have we realized our objectives, our *leitmotif*?

We can also recognize an inner dynamic within the human seven-year rhythm. To begin with, there is an initial period of about two years until the actual laws of the seven-year-period make themselves felt. In the following three years we are at the centre of the seven-year-period and its laws. The last two years are used to review what we have experienced and prepare for the next phase which is already making itself felt from the future. Past, present and future work hand-in-hand.

We might also examine the individual years of the seven-year-period from the perspective of planetary effects. Here, too, we pass through the various planetary spheres of influence in an order which comprises Moon, Mercury, Venus, Sun, Mars, Jupiter and Saturn. The Sun year always brings the new element in the seven-year-period. Beredene Jocelyn assigns the years after 63 to Uranus, Neptune and Pluto. The forces of these planets, too, affect human beings, even if in a looser and lesser way.

What are the major thresholds in the three great phases of our life, if looked at in their tripartite nature? They are readiness for school at seven, puberty at 14, and coming of age at 21. Our physical body originates on earth. It contains our hereditary predisposition and it matures in three great stages: the central nervous system (brain and spinal cord) matures in the first seven-year-period. The respiratory and circulatory system matures in the second seven-year-period; and the limbs (growth, strengthening of bones, muscles and tendons), metabolic system (all glands and the digestive system now become fully active), and our reproductive organs mature in the third seven-year-period. We have already explained this in detail in previous chapters. When we refer to the *process of maturing*, it means that the relevant organs have become fully developed and can be used from that moment onwards as instruments for our soul and spiritual development. The soul is able to play its physical instrument, as it were, once the organs have matured, and unfolds as a thinking, feeling and willing being.

Our personality is spiritual in origin and penetrates deeper and deeper into the physical body from birth onwards. In this context we might speak of three smaller births of the 'I.' The moment when the nervous and sensory system has completely developed in the middle of the first seven-year-period and the child calls itself 'I' for the first time, may be described as the awakening of ego-consciousness. The child feels for the first time that I and the world are not one. Then the child goes through its difficult years when it asserts itself more strongly. In the second seven-year-period, at around the age of nine or ten, the feelings gradually awaken as the rhythmical system (heart and lungs) matures. It is a phase in which children become more inward to a certain extent and somewhat dreamy, but also display more aggression towards parents and teachers. We might describe this as ego-feeling. In the middle of the third seven-year-period, at about 18½, the 'I' penetrates deeply into the metabolic and limb system and young people experience their own activity in the world. This is the phase when they become firmly grounded. Frequently this is also the time when they gain an insight into their talents as regards an occupation. We might describe this process as 'the awakening of the "I" in its global social context.' It is the task of educators to help young people in the first three seven-year-periods gain a solid foothold and to ensure that they are physically healthy — *mens sana in corpore sano*. If the educator is successful, we can say of the young person: 'He is well incarnated.' or: 'He is firmly engaged in his body.' Young people are not fully present until they are 21. At that point they can make use of every single part of the body. The 'I' is no longer occupied to such an extent with building up the body and becomes liberated — the young person comes of age.

The dynamics of the respective organ systems are mirrored

intensively on a soul level. In the first seven-year-period we live completely in our perception of the world, every influence comes from outside. In the second seven-year-period we feel the dynamics of the cardio-pulmonary system. There is constant breathing in and breathing out, contraction and expansion. There is lively interchange between inside and outside, outside and inside. In the third seven-year-period the dynamism of our will is transferred from the inside to the outside. We are active from the inside and help to form our human environment. These dynamics are repeated in the middle phase of our life. They consist essentially of absorption, assimilation and exchange as well as handing things on and transformation.

At this point, let us skip the middle phase of life and turn to the rhythms and reflections in the three seven-year-periods of spiritual development, the time from 42 to 63. For we will see here the reflection of the first three seven-year-periods. Human beings are now in a phase in which the personality gradually begins to separate from the physical body. We might describe this as an 'excarnation process.' Figure 8 (page 145) shows this with a rising line. The excarnation process does not take place from the head to the feet, like the incarnation process, but in reverse order from the feet to the head. From 42 to 49 the forces of the metabolic and limb system begin to withdraw. What can we observe in this respect? The muscles become weaker, in women menstruation ceases at the end of this phase. The body which has been transformed in this way begins to run wild by itself if this process happens too rapidly or if the incarnation in the abdominal area went badly in youth. On the other hand, the withdrawal of these organic forces releases a new creativity. During this phase we mirror the period from 14 to 21 on an organic level. The forces of the rhythmical system, heart and lungs, withdraw from 49 to 56. A new, slower rhythm of life must be found which takes account of our physical degeneration. Now the asthmatic crises of childhood often return or we suffer from heart disease. Here we reflect the period from seven to fourteen.

What new ability in the soul and spiritual realm is enabled by the withdrawal of these forces? We can develop a new feeling for the moral element, for ethics. We become sensitive to the requirements of humankind. It has a beneficial and health-giving effect on our cardiac and pulmonary system if we can manage to develop our soul in this spirit. That does not, of course, mean that we are unable to develop such powers in earlier years. But we are only ripe for such a development from a physiological perspective at this time. The forces of the nervous and sensory system withdraw from 56 to 63. As we already mentioned, our sensory organs are no longer as sharp. This phase of our life mirrors the first seven-year-period in which these organs developed. If too much vitality was used for the intellect, perhaps by a learning process which started too early, then the risk of premature sclerosis arises at this point — unless preventive measures were taken.

What organ of perception can our soul acquire in these years? We are able increasingly to perceive our 'I' as a spiritual reality, as a mirror of the spiritual nature of the cosmos. This is a phase when we very much turn inwards.

If at the time of the first three seven-year-periods the forces of incarnation did not lead to harmonious organic development — the causes for this may be due to heredity, education or destiny — the excarnating forces will find it difficult now to withdraw from the body completely. It is rather like when we climb over barbed wire and catch our clothing on a barb. Doctors often have to help these forces to disengage harmoniously in this phase. Sometimes medical intervention may even be required.

The experience of the first seven-year-period: 'The world is good,' the second seven-year-period: 'The world is beautiful,' and the third seven-year-period: 'The world is true,' may now return as an intensive experience of truth, beauty and goodness.

We now return to the three middle seven-year-periods, the time of soul development. The 'I' has become liberated in this phase and is able to begin the transformation of what has been

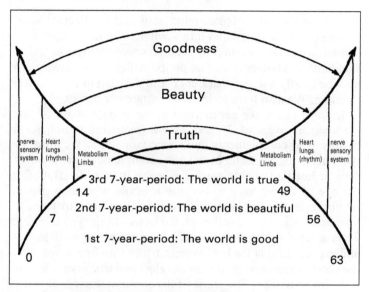

nerve sensory system	Heart lungs (rhythm)	Metabolism Limbs		Metabolism Limbs	Heart lungs (rhythm)	nerve sensory system

Goodness

Beauty

Truth

3rd 7-year-period: The world is true
14   49

2nd 7-year-period: The world is beautiful
7   56

1st 7-year-period: The world is good
0   63

Figure 8. The mirroring of spirit and body.

preserved and learnt in the first 21 years. The 'I' returns to the first three seven-year-periods once more and transforms them. The age of 21 thus becomes a further mirror image in a person's lifestory. Our emotional impulses, which start at 14, are now increasingly brought under control, purified, reined in. The phase of the sentient soul, the age from 21 to 28, is powerfully determined by the preceding stage. Young people mostly start training for an occupation at 16 or 18 which is then brought to completion at 24 or 26. Thereafter they enter work. From 28 to 35 we are in the middle years of our life. At the mid-point of this period, when we are exactly 31½ years old, we have penetrated our body most deeply with our incarnation process. Thereafter a gradual separation begins again. The fifth seven-year-period is also the time when we are most selfish. And our thinking and feelings — Rudolf Steiner calls

this phase the time of the 'mind soul and intellectual soul'
— must now be integrated into a whole. We now experience
similar dynamics as in the second seven-year-period. The
standards and habits from that period which tie us down must
now be finally shed so that our 'I' can develop in ever greater
freedom. We also have to learn to change our habits.

In most cases, we get married in the middle phase of life.
Between the ages of 21 and 28 we frequently search for a
partner who complements us in a certain sense. We fuse the
two halves together and in this way complement one another.
This is justified at that particular stage in our life. But after
the age of 28 we have to become a whole with each person
retaining his or her individual self, and we have to learn to
love and respect one another on the basis of this type of unity.
Thus a relationship which might have been full of demands
and expectations at the beginning can turn into free devotion to
the other person and gradually develop into true comradeship.

From 35 to 42 — the phase of the consciousness soul — we
approach the time when the liberated forces of the body enable
us to reach a higher consciousness. Such a comprehensive
development is only possible if we have developed a healthy
physical body in the first seven-year-period.

Anyone who knows the legend of Parsifal should look at
the lifestories of the individual figures and will be surprised
to find his own soul processes represented there in the form of
images. From a certain point onwards, Parsifal begins to meet
the people he has met before. He has to repeat much in a different form, much arising from the past must be redeemed and
atoned for. The same happens to us in the phases from 21 to 42
until we have finally become fully mature. In our life we will
certainly not have to deal with events which keep repeating
themselves, but we will be confronted with situations which
present themselves in transformation or which take place at a
different level altogether, namely on the soul level. Another
mirror image in the human lifestory occurs at around the age
of 42. It is discussed on p.166.

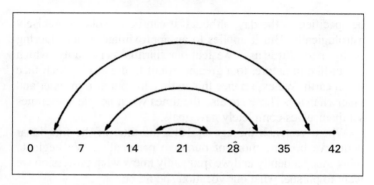

Figure 9. The mirroring of soul development.

If we try to find the place where a mirroring process occurs in our lifestory, we run the risk of trying to anticipate new mirror images. That is a risk because life is a constant metamorphosis and is determined by transformation processes. Thus certain elements may confront us for a second time in a completely different form.

Other rhythms, apart from such mirror images and the seven-year-rhythm, also play an important role in our lifestory. An important rhythm to which we have already repeatedly referred, is the so-called lunar node rhythm. It repeats itself every 18 years and seven months. The point where the paths of the sun and the moon cross traverses the whole of the zodiac in a period of 18 years and seven months. After this exact period the crossing point returns to the place of departure where it was at the time of the birth of the person concerned.

Human life and nature are strongly influenced by the moon. It brings the forces of the past into our present life. Thus its effect is particularly strong in the first seven-year-period, but it continues until the physical body is almost fully developed at the age of 19. What effect do the lunar nodes have on the human soul? We might say that we shed our past at every lunar node and experience a re-birth through the solar power of our 'I.' The occurrence of a lunar node in our lifestory cannot, of course, be specified to the day, although it can be calculated precisely astrologically. But it applies to an approximate period. During such a period it is as if we feel our spiritual personality, which is sun-like in nature, to a greater extent in the tasks which face us on earth. We experience this in dreams, but also in inner and outer changes. These are also the times when people sometimes set themselves completely new goals.

When we reach the age of 18½, the time of the first lunar node, we become more of our own personality. We begin to think independently and we frequently know what profession we want to pursue, what our vocation should be.

The second lunar node, which occurs at around the age of 37, means renewed reflection about our work. We face the question: how are we to move forward into the future? Here, too, we shed something of the past. Another way of describing lunar nodes is to say that they open the gates of heaven once more and allow us to sense our intentions from before birth again. If everything in our life was still in the nature of preparation up to that point, we now begin to feel our actual vocation much more strongly and we also possess the maturity as people to turn it into reality in the world. That is why it happens so frequently that we change our work at this point or that we only realize then what our real task on earth should be.

The third lunar node, which we pass through at approximately the age of 55½, brings us face to face with the question: how have we made our mark as an individual 'I' in the world? What new tasks relating to humanity do we want to begin? What lies within our powers if our physical forces are perhaps not as resilient as they were?

It becomes clear from most lifestories, that people have difficulty in recalling the time when they were 18½. External changes often take place at this age: starting at university, a journey, and so on. These exercise considerable influence over a person's life. The thirty-seventh year, the second lunar node, stands out with all people and is experienced as a marked change, particularly in respect of inner values. The fifty-sixth year, the time of the third lunar node, almost coincides with the transition from one seven-year-period to the next. Here we ask the question: What have I achieved? What is still to come as a new task or new opportunity?

It can, incidentally, be observed in some lifestories that half the period of a lunar node, about nine years, also forms a certain rhythm.

Another important rhythm in the human lifestory is the Saturn rhythm. It is repeated every 29½ years. That is when the planet returns to the constellation of our birth. Saturn stands in polar opposition to the Moon and is connected with the spiritual moulding of our 'I.' It gives us spiritual guidance for our life. In my own life I experienced greater change between 59 and 60 than at 56. This may vary from one lifestory to another. We may speak of three great phases in the Saturn rhythm as well. There is a preparatory phase to about the age of 30. A second phase follows — from 30 to 60 — when our leitmotifs or intentions are realized. And from 60 onwards we look back on our life and prepare for the future.

There are still other rhythms which we can discover in a person's lifestory, such as the Jupiter rhythm. Jupiter returns to the constellation of our birth every 12 years. Thus the period of 12, 24, 36, etc. represents a repeating rhythm for many people. For some people a rhythm of six years, half the Jupiter rhythm, can also be important. Jupiter brings wisdom, harmony, order into our life. Jesus appears in the Temple in Jerusalem at 12 — and a great change takes place in him at that point which is sensed by his parents. The influence of a new 'I' becomes apparent.

The kind of occupations which they might pursue become apparent in many children at the age of 12. Indeed, some have to start working at that age. Training for an occupation is then generally concluded at 24, and at 36 we are in a position to realize our destiny and fulfil our task on earth. Saturn and Jupiter rhythms coincide at 60: we feel that this is a very special age!

The cycle of 33 years is a completely new rhythm. It is connected with forces of death and resurrection, and thus with the Christ event. We spoke about that earlier. The power of Christ, which has penetrated the earth since the Mystery of Golgotha, works intensively on our 'I.' Our 'I' is of the same spiritual essence as the Christ being. The third year of our life, the ninth, the nineteenth and then the phase from 30 to 33 are particularly related to these Christ forces. And from 33 onwards the power of resurrection can become active in us. That means that we can grasp our lifestory with a new inner strength. Historical events often display a rhythm of 33 years. It is decisive for human evolution.

Furthermore, we repeat the 'lifestory' of humankind as a whole in the development of consciousness in our individual lives. If we compare our individual development and the milestones in the historical development of humankind, then humanity is currently in the phase from 35 to 42, as it were, that is, the phase in which a person develops the consciousness soul. We have to work on ourselves to do that. If we do not do such work we only reach the stage of the sentient soul, up to the age of 28. And we can see many people who have never reached beyond the phase from 21 to 28 in their soul development. They remain completely dependent on their environment and on the opinions of others and they are in constant emotional flux. We become loners in later phases of our life, that is from the age of 42 onwards — humankind in its development as a whole has not yet reached that stage — and the qualities which we are able to develop in this period lie far in advance of the development of humankind. That is why the experience of loneliness occurs so frequently at this age. It is important, however, that seeds for the future development of humankind are laid in a person's individual development.

PART TWO

An Approach to Lifestory Work

7. Methodology

Having gained an insight into the way a life develops, we are now ready to work on our own lifestory. There are various ways of doing this, depending on individual predisposition. We can write down the events of our life consecutively as a story. We can also proceed more systematically by taking a sheet of paper for each seven-year-period and writing down the most important events with their dates if possible. We can fold this paper in half lengthways and write the external events on one side and our feelings on the other. What are external events? The birth of a brother or sister, for example, the death of a grandmother, moves to another house or another country; the first time we went to school, when was our first memory and of what, and so on. We can write our feelings on the right-hand side of the sheet: What kind of relationship did I have with my father and mother? Or what did I feel when my little sister was born? We do this for each seven-year-period.

We can also take a large sheet which is divided into three both vertically and horizontally. This gives us nine fields in which events can be noted. We proceed as follows:

I write the events from age one to 21 in the three left fields from the top downwards and when I get to 21 I go up again in the middle fields from bottom to top. In this way we get the mirror images — we have called them mirror images of the soul — of the first seven-year-period in the sixth, the second in the fifth and the third in the fourth. What might I discover by this means? I might discover that an inexplicable major depression at around the age of 33 is connected with the loss of my grandmother or my mother when I was nine. Or I might see, for example, that I stopped painting, at which I was very

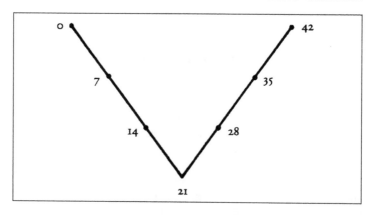

Figure 10. Mirror images of the soul.

talented, at 14 and at 28 I suddenly have the urge to start painting again. If I am older than 42 I use the third column on the right which is meant for the period from 42 to 63 and also proceed from bottom to top (see Figure 11).

Writing down the events in our life is a therapeutic act in itself. It helps us to form and order our thoughts. If we look at our diary in later years we are often surprised about ourselves. There are many things we do not see until we look at them from a distance. Thus I would advise everyone to write down their lifestory — in the form of a diary or on single sheets arranged in order of time. The key events in our life can easily be inserted into this kind of framework.

When I set the outer events of my life and my emotions next to one another on a 'lifestory sheet,' I can see the reflection of the time up to 21 in the period from 42 to 63 as well. Here too we can sometimes experience strange events. For example I experience a great urge at 47 to build a swimming pool. Where does it come from? It cannot really be explained. If I look back to when I was 16 I can see that I was an active swimmer at that time and trained a lot. Another example. I suddenly realize at 54 that my asthma is returning, which I have not had since I was nine.

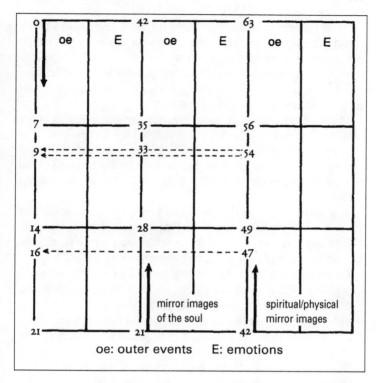

Figure 11. Biography Sheet.

I can also try to work on an emotional level. I could give the various seven-year-periods different colours: say, yellow for great happiness or dark blue for acute depressive states, and so on. I can then see which colours correspond to which in the mirror image. Each person can be creative here and decide how they want to proceed. Such a list on the lifestory sheet also allows us to discover which events are repeated in a different form. One man noticed, for example, that he changed jobs every nine years. Now he is in a nine-year cycle for the third time and notices that everything is getting more difficult for him at work. But since he has changed jobs twice already, he says to himself now: 'I have a tendency to change jobs every nine years. But this time I want to avoid a repeat of previous situations.' He therefore tries to tackle the difficulties which have arisen at the workplace. He feels after a while that his endeavours are bringing success.

I have also noticed, for example, that the same elements are being repeated in my present marriage which I experienced in a previous one. And by consciously becoming aware of that, I can work on those elements. Perhaps divorce can be avoided this time because I try to tackle and resolve the problems from the inside.

A young woman notices that she keeps falling in love, that men are often attracted to her. Is that due to her or to the men? The young woman has to ask herself: 'Do I want to change that situation, or do I want it to keep repeating itself?'

Or I notice suddenly that I treat my children in the exact same way that my father used to treat me and my brothers and sisters. Yet I felt strongly the pain, the damage which he caused me. Will I continue to use him as a model or do I attempt to cultivate my own relationship and ways of living with my children?

A man looking back on his lifestory might notice that he did not have any youth because he had to start working and bear responsibilities at an early age. He also married very early. Now he is a little over 40 and his children, especially his eldest son, are already teenagers. The son has many girlfriends and owns a motorbike. He is happy and enjoys himself. Memories of his lost youth now arise in the father; he is jealous of his son in a certain sense. He, too, would like to be free once more like his son and go for drives with various girlfriends. He would like to leave home, feel free and live through this youth phase once more. How do we handle such feelings in practice? Do we let ourselves drift along without restraint or do we attempt to transform our jealousy and develop a better understanding of the son and his generation? Would it not be better to feel happiness that the son has the opportunity to experience in his teenage years what was denied to us? Many people talk about what they have missed in life, but basically they have not missed anything, for while they were studying or working they replaced what they think they have 'missed' with something else. We cannot be in two places at the same time, say in America and Europe. If we lived in Europe we need not have the feeling later that we 'missed' America. For we learnt a great deal in Europe which we could not have done in America.

We have to learn to pay attention to the opportunities which come our way in life and to ask whether we have used them properly, whether we are happy with the outcome. Many people are constantly unhappy with themselves because they feel in the wrong place with regard to the situation in which they happen to find themselves. Often they dream what it would be like if they were somewhere else. This causes a feeling of dissatisfaction. Such people think that they have to catch up on something. We do, indeed, have to catch up on some things — the issue, however, is the way in which we do it. Is it appropriate for a 42-year-old man to behave like his 18-year-old son, or are there other ways in which he could make up what he feels he has 'missed' which are more appropriate to his age? Could he not catch up in a transformed way?

Now that we have an oversight over our life, and its events are spread out before us, there are further steps we can take. In a lifestory course we might, for example, try to give expression to our lifestory in artistic form once we have written it down from memory. We can try to do this by painting, or by modelling if we have the aptitude and time for that, perhaps in the following way:

We paint a picture for every seven-year-period. If we have achieved a comprehensive view of the seven-year-period we can put this down on paper in symbols or colours. Or we can take a scene or incisive experience from the seven-year-period and try to express it in shape or colour. We have included Figures 12a–c as examples. The course participant who made them chose a symbolic form for each of the first three seven-year-periods. The originals were done in water-colour. They were turned into sketches for this book. The series of Figures 13 a–d (pages 160f) and 14 a–d (pages 162f) express concrete experiences. We explain to the participants at lifestory courses that the important thing is not how beautiful the pictures turn out; the participants should, rather, observe their inner feelings while they are painting.

It is obvious from the series of picture in Figure 13 that the participant is a business manager. He was fascinated by mechanical things from his earliest years. Figure 13a: the horse and carriage made a deep impression on the participant as a child! In Figure 13b, he builds a water-pump by himself at the age of eight — suddenly his mother has a water supply in the kitchen! In Figure 13c he owns a small farm, but he is already thinking about a factory, which is shown in the lower part of the picture. In Figure 13d he succeeds in building the factory and he feels that he has fully realized his plans.

It is obvious that the young woman who painted the series of pictures in Figure 14 was born in the city (São Paolo), married and built up a happy family.

The next step in a lifestory course is that participants form a group. They sit down together voluntarily and talk about their lifestories. They may use their pictures and their notes for this, but should try to draw on their memory when they are telling their story. In our courses we work with groups of three, four or five, but not more than seven. It is important that participants should recreate the key elements in their life while they are telling their lifestory. But in doing so, it is left up to each participant to tell the things which he or she thinks important and, above all, only to tell those things which he or she is willing to impart voluntarily.

The result of such group work is that the telling of a lifestory brings out hidden memories and feelings in the others. They awaken inwardly, as it were, and gain a better insight

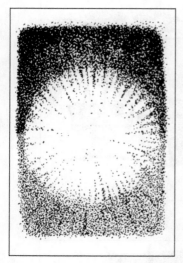

a

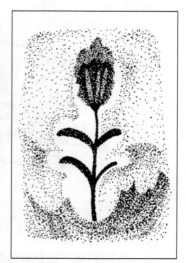

b

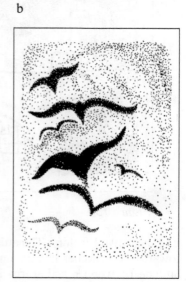

*Figure 12. Spontaneous
symbolic images of the first
three seven-year periods.
a: first seven-year-period
b: second seven-year-period
c: third seven-year-period*   c

Figure 13a.

Figure 13b.

into their own lifestory. The attitude of the course participants towards one another is very important. We try to develop an attitude of wonder and warm interest within the group. We experience each person as master of their own lifestory, tackling

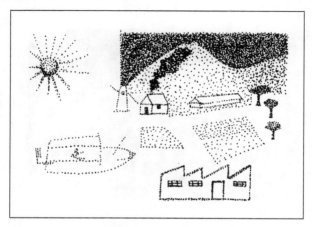

Figure 13c.

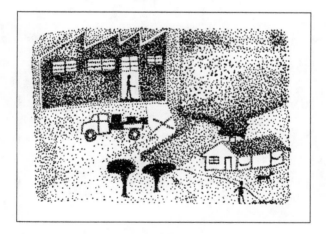

Figure 13d.

his or her problems. Questions may then be used to bring even greater clarity into the consciousness of the other. We have to learn to listen to our fellow human beings, to be attentive, to recognize and understand what wants to come out and be

Figure 14a.

Figure 14b.

revealed in the words. That is one aspect. The other is that we should try to express ourselves as clearly as possible and to formulate our language in such a way that it is accessible to the others, that they understand us. It is also important to not

Figure 14c.

Figure 14d.

be too side-tracked by details and diversions, so that we end up talking about our father or brother instead of ourselves. On the contrary, we should concentrate on ourselves when telling our lifestory. We try to create an atmosphere of warmth, of cosiness in such group work which makes all the participants feel safe. Although they experience their limits, the openness with which people mostly speak in the group makes the participants feel that they can trust the others. The more openly participants speak in a group, the more this helps to deepen the lifestory work.

Every participant is given a set time to which he or she should adhere as far as possible. The group takes on the task of acknowledging and listening to the other, it forms the mirror and receptacle for the person who narrates his or her life to the group. The narrator, in turn, enriches the group with his life experience and thus the group also takes on the role of recipient. When some people tell their lifestory to the group it may be necessary to keep linking elements of the past with the present. The group must attempt to avoid any expression of criticism or of explanation of the lifestory which has been presented.

Sometimes the groups work on their own. Most of the groups which we look after in 'Artemisia' are accompanied by a moderator. His only purpose really is to keep a check on the time and to help the smooth running of the group work by asking questions.

The same work which has been described here for a group of participants can also be done with a single person — in the form of a conversation between patient and therapist. Each person can even do it on their own.

Our seminars last from four to seven days. This gives us the opportunity to divide up the time. Either we deal with two seven-year-periods on a day or we work with one of the major phases in life. This is done both in connection with the large sheet on which we have written down the events of our life and with the painting exercises and group conversations. We must have reached the present by the second last day. With the painting we can proceed as before, or we can set the task of painting a new picture which represents the present situation of the course participant. If we proceed with the painting as previously, a specific scene or symbol is chosen which characterizes the present situation. On the last day of the course the participants then attempt to express their future in the painting exercise. They do this from the point of view: Where do I want to go from here? What does the landscape of my life look like in the future?

If we want to add a new exercise, we can let the person concerned represent himself in the form of a plant with which he identifies. Then the picture is passed around the small group with the request that the other participants add little 'gifts' to the picture by the person concerned. They might, for example, add the sun or rain, colourful flowers on the grass, a gardener watering the plants, or people surrounding him, and so on (see the series of drawings in Figure 15a–c). The group must not change anything on the plant which the person concerned has drawn himself, only the 'landscape' surrounding the plant may be added to. It is, after all, very simple to criticize others. It is very tempting to try and change them — but to emphasize their value (by drawing the background to the picture) or giving them what they need is a difficult social task. This exercise is particularly designed to practise social abilities. All the participants start from the idea that they would like to give something to the person concerned so that his plant will thrive. Then the group discusses the picture and everyone explains what they have given the other person and why. The person concerned is allowed to say beforehand why he has chosen this particular plant to represent his lifestory. Very interesting things emerge with this exercise and the social element is given a boost.

The gifts for the other person may be accepted and assimilated or not. The next day, when we work on our objectives, our future, these gifts are incorporated and everyone once more paints the plant and the landscape which they want to realize in future. Any interpretation or criticism of the pictures are avoided. In most cases everyone who has painted a picture suddenly gains some new understanding — and this is frequently due to the new perspective which the 'gifts' received have opened up; he begins to notice that he has forgotten to give his tree any roots or that he has positioned his plant right at the side of the picture. In other words, he begins to realize by himself what he might have done better or differently on his picture. Thus the second last day of the course, the 'gift' day, turns into its high point because at this moment the fruits of co-operation in the group become visible. The moments of group work can really bring about the experience: 'When two or three are gathered in my name I am among them.' And this fertilizing element is extraordinarily vitalizing from a therapeutic perspective, for which we should be grateful.

The following exercise may still be added: On the day preceding the day when the course deals with the present situation, every participant tries before going to sleep vividly to imagine the people in his group once more, and to formulate a question for each participant which might help the other to greater awareness. In a group of four each participant would then have three questions. The questions are discussed next day together with the 'picture gifts.' Indeed, it is essential for any work with lifestories that the 'lifestory therapist' is able to ask the right questions.

If we want to gain rapid insight into our lifestory, we can use one of the patterns below instead of the large sheet of paper. The outline on page 154 (Figure 10) is rather more suited to people under the age of 42. It provides an immediate overview of the various mirror images. The outline on page 168 (Figure 16) is suitable for people over the age of 42 as well. It may also be used for the period from 35 onwards. We will find somewhat different elements in the construction of this outline than in the outline in Figure 10. This displays the incarnation process on the one side and the excarnation process on the other. The point of time at 31½ is at the centre of events. It is the point at which we are most deeply linked with our body and the earth. We will notice that many encounters and events occur about this time.

The pattern which uses the age of 42 as the focus of the mirror images can also be of help to us (see Figure 17). Here

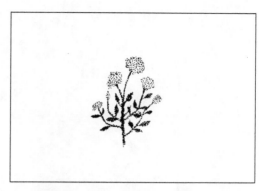

Figure 15a–c.

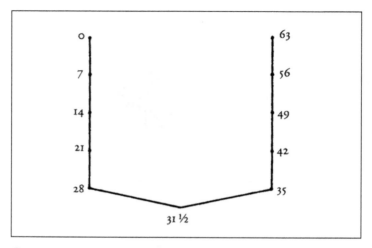

Figure 16. Spiritual and physiological mirror image

we can see how our soul increasingly becomes a mantle for the spirit. This means that we work on the transformation of the various soul elements (sentient soul, mind or intellectual soul and consciousness soul) in such a way from 21 to 42 that the soul becomes a vessel for the spirit. To use an image: Our precious stone, the spirit, is cut in such a way that from the age of 42 to 63 it reflects with full clarity the spiritual and cosmic element and that the imaginative, inspirative and intuitive soul can develop from these soul elements.

We have also developed other forms of lifestory work at 'Artemisia,' for those who have already attended the introductory course. The same template is used, but now it is not the events of one's life which are entered, but the encounters which one has had. This type of work leads to the insight that our own destiny and personality have been formed by the people whom we meet in life. Questions arise such as: How has this or that person influenced my destiny from birth up to the present moment?

We proceed in our work as suggested by Rudolf Steiner in his lecture of 12 December 1918, 'Social and Anti-Social

Forces in the Human Being', in combination with an exercise. We try to create an image of the course participant and to observe it free of any antipathy or sympathy. Then we can draw a cosmos in which we place all the people with whom we have any sort of relationship at the present moment. We mark which people are close to us, which ones not so close. In this way we can express whether these relationships are of a physical, spiritual or soul nature, whether it is a work relationship, and so on. We can become very creative here and an overview of this image of human relations enables us to take many new decisions. We can also discover which relationships have died and are simply being maintained on an outward level. If we want to start new relationships in the future we probably have to make some room so that these new stars can enter our life. That, too, is an important objective.

We have already described the exercise in which we draw a tree and observe which branches have withered and have to be pruned and what the buds mean which are developing for the future.

It can also be a further objective to return to the old relationships once more and to bring them into harmony and balance.

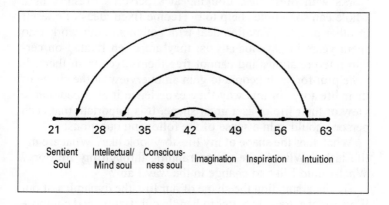

Figure 17.

That has proved particularly fruitful with people who are seriously ill and who feel that something remains to be settled in their destiny. If that is possible, many of these people can look on the end of their life in greater peace.

The artistic exercise in this advanced form of work on one's own lifestory can take the following form:

We use a large sheet of paper to draw our whole lifestory in the shape of a river which flows through various landscapes. Sometimes it may even disappear underground in order to resurface later. It flows through mountains, valleys, through dry deserts, and so on. Then we can add the people whom we encountered on our way. Depending on the nature of our encounters, we can draw them as human figures or as symbols. We can also give them the shape of a characteristic plant. This too provides insights and helps us to look more profoundly at our lifestory and achieve greater objectivity about the events of our life.

We also like to set the task of transforming our own lifestory into a fairy tale. This sometimes produces very nice results, such as the lifestory in the form of a fairy tale which is printed on page 124. It is another tool for the therapist who works with lifestories. Looking at a person's lifestory as a whole can sometimes help to overcome fixed ideas of oneself or other people. We often deal with patients in our work who spent years in psychoanalysis; they are often fixated on certain interpretations and cannot free themselves from them. It is helpful for such people to gain an overview of the shape of their lifestory. In this way they experience it as a panoramic view of their life or as a great shape. It is important that each person should gain a sense of the following questions:

What does the shape of my lifestory look like? What are my life tasks? What is the thread running through my lifestory? What would I like to change in the way I am?

By understanding the shape of our life, the dynamics of our lifestory, we are able better to handle our destiny and compose our whole life into an unfinished symphony.

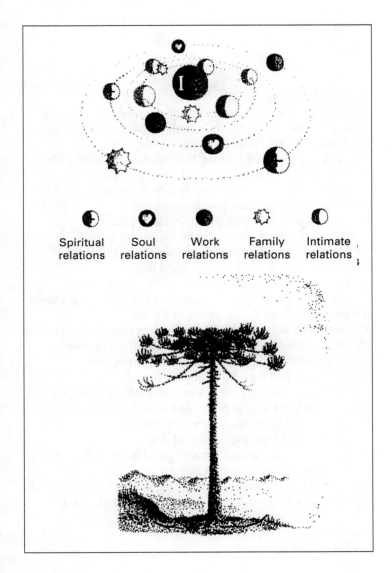

Spiritual   Soul   Work   Family   Intimate
relations   relations   relations relations   relations

Figure 18.

The cosmic pilgrim
When once I'm carried out don't say: 'Eternal rest' –
Put in my grave, with pilgrim's clothes, two walking shoes.
Three days I'll rest. Then I'll be on my way.
Here glaciers and there burning heat: narrow the spirit path.
The mountain air is good, soon I'll be well again.
My steps go, liberated from the earth, to starry planes.
I wore an earthly garment which was soiled.
The moon's own dew will quickly make it pure.
Walking along the penitential path, the silvery track –
Mercury lends my steps his winged shoes.
My tiredness gives way to happy spirit flight
As Venus shines with grace and gives the pilgrim youth.
Like fire of resurrection of the rose, like lily's purity of a child
The human soul enters the portals of the Sun.
A gesture from the angel of the Sun: receive your spear and shield!
The spacious fields of Mars call you to fight the cosmic war.
If you, a human spirit, wish to rouse the cosmic one –
Jupiter's shine will serve to light your flame!
The unifier of death and life, Saturn guards the eternal hoard,
The silence ripens to give birth: 'In the beginning was the Word.'
The cosmic words resounds from stars profound
To free the spirit from the bounds of death.
Thus grows the human spirit, transfigured by the light of God,
Until, driven by love, it returns to earth.
He does not know 'Eternal peace' — the pilgrim's clothes for him,
A pair of walking boots: ready to walk the path of destiny!

Rudolf Meyer

8. Motivation for life: setting objectives

Each person faces the questions: What motivates my life? What are my duties? What is my mission? What abilities do I possess? What difficulties do I have to fight with? Why do certain situations keep recurring in my life? What is the thread running through my life?

We are unlikely to be able to answer these questions if we do not recognize that we are the inhabitants of two worlds, a physical world and the world of heaven, of the spirit. On the one hand we have our biological body, which is physical in nature and determined by heredity. On the other hand a higher 'I' inhabits us which is spiritual in nature. And just as our inherited characteristics are determined by a long line of ancestors — many people still like to have their family tree drawn up, even today — so our 'I' also has a long line of antecedents. They are partly linked with the earth (this is what we describe as incarnation) and partly with the cosmos. We can compare the time in the cosmos with the seed which rests in the earth in winter and waits for spring in order to sprout and grow. Or we can compare it with a river which flows partially under the earth and is thus invisible to us. Rudolf Steiner put the teachings about reincarnation into a form appropriate for modern consciousness and they can be found in many of his books.*

The physical and spiritual streams of human existence are united at conception and birth. The personality prepares for its physical existence over a long period in the cosmos, where it is still at a spiritually embryonic stage. The hereditary stream supplies the characteristics of the physical constitution. As embryonic spirits, we search for the hereditary line which offers us the kind of physical constitution which we are

* *See* Metamorphoses of the Soul; Manifestations of Karma *and* Reincarnation and Karma.

able to utilize as a physical instrument for realizing our spiritual intentions here on earth. If, for example, it is part of my intention to develop my genius on earth in the form of music, I have to choose a body which offers me good hearing, among other things. Or if I want to work as a doctor I have to find a family which will offer me that opportunity.

The 'I' brings intentions with it from before birth which it wants to realize on earth. In addition, it brings certain predispositions from its cosmic existence so that it can put its intentions into practice. Some of these predispositions come from the zodiac — whether I am born under Sagittarius or Cancer will make a considerable difference to my stance in life. Other predispositions come from the sphere of the planets. I might bring Mars qualities with me which give me entrepreneurial abilities, or Saturn qualities which encourage me to get to the root of matters and give me investigative characteristics, to name but a few examples (see Bernard Lievegoed's books in the Bibliography.) Other predispositions are connected with the temperaments. My temperament might owe more to the element of fire, water, air, or earth.

We, as individuals, thus bring with us the predispositions which we have acquired as a result of the influence of the following four spheres: the zodiac, the planetary sphere, the elements and our physical constitution (heredity). Those are four strings on an instrument, as it were, which our personality can play freely to allow its life music to resound. They are innate characteristics which enable the personality to implement here on earth its reason for living.

These are the predispositions which we bring with us; then, however, we encounter the external circumstances into which we are born: our environment, country, language, home, family, teachers and school, society, culture and period. All these conditions contribute to the development of our personality. Thus we set out on life at the age of 21, well equipped, find our partner, job, and meet other people who can help us to grow psychologically.

Gradually, once we are beyond 30, our intentions in life increasingly come to be realized. Until that time we should concentrate particularly on developing our skills. Whether we succeed in this, and whether we can feel that we have realized our personality, depends, of course, on our inner strength and persistence, as well as on the greater and lesser external obstacles we encounter.

Life on earth increasingly turns our gifts into abilities. Many of them we produced just like that. These are the ones which our 'I' brings along from previous incarnations. Other abilities have to be laboriously worked at.

We have already mentioned how our skills have to be transformed from the inside at about 28. We leave some capabilities behind and others are changed in order to make them fruitful for humankind. We fulfil our tasks and transform our abilities in the process. We are in the great phase of life of 'being human.' Everything which we encounter must be practised and learned, particularly as regards handling the difficulties and obstacles connected with work and relationships. Each one of us has experienced the way in which something we have learnt laboriously on one day — perhaps a few new words in a foreign language or a piece on the piano — appears the next day as a transformed ability. Everything becomes much easier. Every learning process is based on this transformation — practice creates new abilities. Not everything which we practice in life succeeds, however. But it is important to know that the effort which we make is not lost, but is stored, as it were, and if it does not bear fruit later in life, it will do so in our next incarnation. If we have consciously developed our phase of 'human fulfilment' we can look to the future with greater riches, particularly in old age, for this creates new abilities, new motivation, new skills for the next incarnation. Just as night occurs between days, and many things are transformed from one day to the next during sleep, there is also a cosmic night in which things we have practised, our lived and processed experiences, are transformed into new gifts, abilities and motivation. We can speak about a day-time lifestory — this is the part which we accompany with our consciousness — and a night-time lifestory which we cannot grasp with our ordinary day-time consciousness. We only get an overview after death (the start of the great cosmic night) when we experience the continuity of our lifestory as a whole.

People who are close to drowning or who have experienced other types of shock (being buried, an operation, or similar) sometimes experience a panoramic view of their life. Their whole life flashes before them in seconds. After death, too, each person lives through a phase in which he or she has a panoramic view of their life once more. Then they pass through kamaloca (or purgatory) and the various planetary spheres. This is described in many of Rudolf Steiner's works.* The individual phases after death have a direct effect on the life of a person in the next incarnation. As we have already explained, the seven-year rhythm is the result of our self having passed through the planetary spheres between death and a new birth. The influence of the various planetary forces then makes itself felt in the different phases of life (see p.140).

The more consciously we gain an overview while we are alive of the way our life has developed, the more consciously we can understand after death the fruits of our life and our mistakes, and work on our future with other forces. For what we have acquired on earth can be transformed after death. In the period of kamaloca we form the impulse to rectify the harm we have done to another person. And this creates the necessity of another encounter with that person in a new life.†

If we look at our encounters from the perspective of what each person means to us in life, we gain greater clarity in developing our relationships. Past and future always shake

---

* *See* Karmic Relationships; An Outline of Occult Science *and* Theosophy.

† *See Steiner,* Karmic Relationships; Manifestations of Karma *and* Reincarnation and Karma.

hands, and just as the past determines our path through life on the one hand, so the future makes its mark on the course of our life on the other. A crisis in life must always be looked at from this perspective. Is it something that comes from the past or does it represent uncertainties which come from the future? For a crisis in life can happen because the future is already unconsciously exerting its influence; I feel the changes which I must make and bring about, but I am still constrained by earlier situations.

Thus when we examine the present moment, elements both from the past and from the future may be at work. Both are unconscious. We can attempt to make them increasingly part of our consciousness. If we succeed, we are, after all, in a better position to develop our future objectives in a more conscious way.

The following verse from Rudolf Steiner provides a nice conclusion to this topic:

> The wishes of the soul are springing
> The deeds of the will are thriving
> The fruits of life are maturing.
>
> I feel my fate,
> My fate finds me.
> I feel my star,
> My star finds me.
> I feel my goals in life,
> My goals in life are finding me.
>
> My soul and the great World are one.
>
> Life grows more radiant about me,
> Life grows more arduous for me,
> Grows more abundant within me.

(from *Verses and Meditations*)

9. Guide for setting personal objectives

Once we have worked on our life as it has developed in the past, we have to be quite clear about the present time so that we are able to picture our objectives quite clearly.

It is a good exercise, for example, to ask where we see ourselves in ten years' time. This often forces us to think about the future and inquire into our real objectives. Our motivation in life is linked to our objectives. Someone who has no objectives in life has no pleasure in life. People who are in a depression, whose life might appear empty or has become too much of a routine, can be helped to find new objectives. This work can also be of great help to someone with a serious illness or to a dying person.

There are short, medium and longer term objectives. There are objectives for the various areas of our life. What might they look like? We give some examples and guidelines for the individual spheres:

1. The economic sphere:
– our salary
  For example: I will use 20% of my salary for cancer research.
– our possessions
  What acquisitions are we still going to make?
  How will we divide our possessions later (will)?

2. Health objectives:
  Start homeopathic treatment, for example, do sport or change something in my diet.

3. Work objectives:
– How will my career develop in the future?
– What is my real task, my mission?

For example: I want to teach young joinery students as well as doing my engineering job.

4. Relationships:
- family relationships
- professional relationships
  For example: Cultivate a better relationship with my boss in order to avoid conflict and tensions. How do I go about this in a concrete way?
- friendships
- partner

5. Objectives of self-development:
- of a spiritual kind:
  Work on the exercises of a path of schooling for example. Say a prayer, practice meditation; or resume my belief; or learn about a new philosophy of life.
- of a psychological kind:
  Work on my impatience, my arrogance for example.
- of a practical kind:
  Learn to cook better; or learn to draw better.

6. Objectives of humankind:
I would like to contribute something to the ecology of my country for example; or to research into dementia; or to the path of development of human beings.

We can also classify objectives into:

- **objectives of survival**
- **objectives of self-realization**
- **objectives of self-development**
- **objectives of humankind**

It goes without saying that the various levels are interrelated and that the order used above is only meant as an aid for working on the objectives.

10. Working on your own lifestory

Apart from a list of events (good and bad) from the individual phases of life, the following questions and points of view can be helpful in finding the thread running through each section of life:

Up to age 7:
– my first memory
– my first sensory impressions
– my home and its environment, and the people living in it
– relationships with my father, mother, siblings, great grand-parents. What profession did they have?
– games

From age 7 to 14:
– school, teachers, educational methods
– standards and habits which were inculcated in me
– what was my religious education like?
– my artistic activities (music, painting, drama, handwork, handicrafts, sculpting, etc.)
– opportunities for sport, excursions, experiences of nature
– opportunities for holidays
– was there something special about the tenth year?
– and the twelfth year?
– what changes took place in the run-up to puberty? How did I experience these changes?

From 14 to 21:
– did I develop as a person in this phase or was I prevented from fulfilling my intentions?
– did I have a private space physically and psychologically?
– what were my ideals? Who were my heroes?

- what people exercised a strong influence on me during this period, both positively and negatively?
- how did I choose my job? Was the time at age 18½ a special one?
- did I have opportunities for further education?

From 21 to 28:
- did I choose the right job?
- did I have the opportunity to get to know various work places?
- did I have a variety of work experience?
- did I have a good boss?
- what roles did I assume? Was one of them particularly difficult for me?
- what ideals did I have?
- what talents did I abandon (which were not required of me in life)?
- how did I choose my partner?
- did I find a proper relationship to the world, to the organization of which I am part, to myself?

From 28 to 35:
- was I able to develop my personality during this period?
- was I repressed or did I repress others?
- did I find my vocation?
- what was my awareness of life, my feeling of self? How did I find fulfilment in life?
- what significant encounters occurred in the period from 30 to 33?
- did something new happen in my life in this period?

From 35 to 42:
- were new values added to my life?
- was I able to change my life in line with these?
- did I feel a significant change around the age of 37?
- am I on the way to fulfilling my mission?
- have I found and acknowledged the vital issue in my life?

– how do I see myself, how do others see me, what illusions
  did I get rid of during this time?

From 42 to 49:
– in what direction am I developing new creativity?
– new hobbies?
– what have I buried by way of skills and abilities which I can
  bring out again now?
– did I ensure successors in my work?
– am I able to pass on the fruits of my life?

From 49 to 56:
– did I find a new rhythm in life?
– what does my daily, weekly, monthly and yearly rhythm
  look like?
– what is the dead wood in my tree which must be pruned for
  new branches to sprout?

From 56 to 63:
– how do I see my lifestory as a whole? What is the thread
  running through my lifestory?
– what was I able to realize? What tasks remain which I
  would still like to realize?
– how do I deal with my physical ailments?
– what can I do to look after my body, and in particular my
  senses and memory?
– are there relationships which remain unresolved? Is there
  anything I can still make up?
– what is the situation regarding my possessions?

From 63 upwards:
– what do I still want to learn in future?
– what new dimensions of consciousness are opening up for me?
– do I feel grace, thankfulness, cheerfulness?
– do I succeed in preserving some forces from childhood and
  youth? How?

11. The author's lifestory

To conclude our examination of lifestory work and its underlying laws, I wish to present my own lifestory. I have written
it as a gesture of gratitude and as a small gift in return for all
the many people who entrusted their lifestories to me and who
thus made this book possible in the first place.

*Both my parents come from Germany. My father came from
Berlin. After the First World War he completed a physiotherapy training course there; he emigrated to Brazil in 1920.
To begin with, he worked in a physiotherapy institute in São
Paolo, from where he went on to found his own institute in
the centre of São Paolo city. My mother comes from an area
which is part of Poland today. My father asked her to come
from Germany in order to marry her without even knowing her
— simply because she was the sister of his sister-in-law. One
year after their marriage my parents separated. My father's
mother had also come from Europe to Brazil before my birth.*

*I spent the first eight months of my life at a lake outside São
Paolo. There we had nature in its magnificence, pure water
and clear air. Even when I was small the whole family bathed
naked in the lake. My mother breast fed me until the ninth
month. My father worked in the city centre and only came back
at the weekends. I do not know the reasons for my parents'
divorce, but I imagine that my mother felt very isolated. She is
also said to have been very jealous.*

*From the age of two onwards I was brought up by my
grandmother and my father. Here my grandmother completely
assumed the maternal role. We moved to a quarter of São
Paolo which was not so distant from the city centre but was
nevertheless surrounded by nature and wilderness. The cows
came up to our fence to eat the rubbish. We were frequently*

visited by very large lizards and a snake which slithered on to our land from a neighbouring property. I had complete freedom to roam the garden and in the summer was mostly naked. We built a large sandpit behind the house which filled with water when it rained. It was pure bliss for me to splash about in it.

I received no vaccinations and no medicines. When I became ill my father wrapped me up in warm blankets so that I sweated out the illness.

I grew up completely with the German language during my childhood.

My step-mother joined us when I was four-and-a-half. I still remember the wedding. My step-mother and father were followers of Mazdaznan at the time, a Persian teaching which is essentially based on sun worship. Every Sunday we drove to the lodge. From that time I still remember the beautiful singing which was cultivated there and which was mainly devoted to the sun. I had some contact with children in the lodge but otherwise grew up as a single child. My father was always very proud of me. And my grandmother, I was later told, always spoiled me. I slept in the same room as her. She and my father were reserved in some ways, but very loving in others. My father and I went on long hikes on Sundays, for example.

My step-mother never took a great part in my upbringing. She was a great individualist, an Argentinian of German descent. It was her third marriage and she had never had children before. She possessed a love of nature and plants. When our house was extended she began to cultivate orchids, cacti and rare plants. She also caught the large lizards and looked after them. She also owned a young tabby cat which sat all day in the trees in our garden. When I look back on my first seven-year-period today, I see that my step-mother brought a certain beauty and aesthetics into our house. Above all, she taught me good manners.

During that period, I remember our Christmas holidays at home with particular love and pleasure. My father had planted

a small wood in the garden and every Christmas he climbed
up the highest tree and cut off the crown as a Christmas tree.

Also of significance for my first seven-year-period was a
female cousin of my step-mother, who came to visit us. I called
her 'Aunt Emma.' She was an anthroposophist and told me
beautiful fairy tales. I developed a deep relationship with this
Aunt Emma, which was to continue in my later life as well.
Incidentally, this aunt also translated Rudolf Steiner's book
Knowledge of the Higher Worlds and its Attainment *into Por-*
tuguese. It was the first translation of any anthroposophical
work into Portuguese. Aunt Emma also wanted to teach me to
play the piano and we got a new piano at this time.

I started school at the age of six. Since I spoke no Portu-
guese, I was going to be sent to a German school in Brazil.
When I went there with my father on the first day of school, I
saw that there was not a single tree in the school playground.
I told my father decisively that I did not want to stay at this
school. He respected my wish. Thus I was sent to a Catholic
convent school which was near our house and which lay
within walking distance. But first I had to learn Portuguese. I
was faced with different problems in the convent school: I had
never been christened. My father wished that I should choose
my religion myself later. The nuns were not happy about that,
of course, and they tried to convert me to their religion for
the whole of my time at school. But they were unsuccessful. I
cultivated my own religion, collected pictures of the saints and
built my own altar at home with stones, candles and plants.

A further problem arose in that I was vegetarian. Since
school was from eight in the morning to five in the afternoon,
I always had to bring my own lunch from home. I remember
that my fellow pupils developed a great interest in my meal
and that I often had to share it with them.

Between the ages of six and 14 I was faced with a new
challenge. Every second year I had to go and visit my
mother. She had initially returned to Germany but had then
moved to Rio de Janeiro. My mother was unwilling to accept

that I was vegetarian and wanted to force me to eat meat. But I was unable to keep such food down and she stopped her attempts. Also, I was used to taking a bath and she insisted that I should take showers. I felt great aggression coming from her and the thought entered my subconscious that if people were angry and aggressive there must be something wrong with them. Thus I had no inner relationship with my mother and my visits only improved once my mother remarried and gave birth to a further two children. After the third child she developed a mental illness and I often had to visit her in the sanatorium. That was psychologically very difficult for me and it took a long time before I was able to deal with psychiatric patients later in life.

A great break in my life occurred at the age of nine. I was run over by a car on the way to swimming lessons. My thorax was completely crushed and I broke fourteen ribs. I can still remember the driver of the car standing over me and looking in my face. I remember that I had to repeat my father's telephone number many times with great difficulty in the ambulance. When I arrived at the first-aid station my father was already there and tried to get me admitted to hospital. But he was told that there was no point since I was going to die anyway. But my father managed to get me into the German hospital with the help of doctor friends. And — wonders will never cease — after three weeks I was fully recovered. My father was very proud of my health and ascribed it to my healthy lifestyle.

At the age of ten I wanted to change schools. I went to a German school in Brazil. But I felt alien there too, for again there were some children who knew that I was vegetarian and a follower of Mazdaznan and who made fun of me. The war had started and teaching in German was forbidden. Some teachers were very strict and often dished out clouts on the ear. I still remember the words: 'Once stupid, always stupid. No remedy for that.' But I did succeed in making friends with several classmates after a time. We went to a sports club together and I began to train in swimming and jumping.

My grandmother died when I was about twelve. My father asked me to put a rose into her hands. I found that very difficult — I realized later why I always avoided helping to prepare the corpses of my deceased patients. I got my own room when my grandmother died. I went on holiday and had the opportunity there to get a glimpse of my future husband. My step-mother did not succeed in exercising any significant influence on my education. I was also away from home a lot. In the morning I went to school and in the afternoon to the sports club. I remained in the sports and swimming club during my youth until the age of 17. We had an excellent Japanese swimming teacher who was a sort of idol for us adolescents. But I continued to be very shy. I did not have boyfriends.

From the age of twelve onwards I knew that I wanted to study medicine. Looking back, I find it hard to judge whether this was my father's wish or my own. I can only say that it was a choice which was proved right by life. I have a great gift for medicine. If the wish came from my father, I am very grateful to him for it.

After another change of school at the age of 14, I gradually began to understand and love chemistry, physics and mathematics, and, of course, biology in particular. I stopped swimming one year before the start of the medical entrance exams and devoted myself completely to my forthcoming studies. The result was that I put on more than ten kilos.

During my time at the German school I developed a great interest in the Protestant religion lessons and at 14 I wanted to be confirmed like my fellow pupils. But my father thought I only wanted to do it for the white dress and the festive event and dissuaded me from going ahead with it.

At 16 I developed a great platonic love for a Chilean swimmer who was twelve years older than I was. It merely came to a lively correspondence.

At 18 I entered medical school. I passed the entrance exams at the first attempt and started my medical studies with great enthusiasm. I found everything fascinating, particularly

anatomy and above all histology. I spent hours at the micro-
scope studying tissue. This led to such a deterioration of my
sight that I had to wear much stronger glasses. I became the
best student in the university in my first six semesters and
received all kinds of awards. Practical work in hospitals
began with the sixth semester. I won the trust of the doctor
in charge and thus I looked after a group of twelve patients
when I was only in fourth year. I also prescribed them medi-
cine. At that time I had stronger ties to my teachers than to
my fellow students.

From my eighteenth year onwards, my parents grew
increasingly interested in anthroposophy. Thus at 21 I came
across a copy of a booklet by Ehrenfried Pfeiffer and I wanted
to undertake some crystallization experiments in my boss's
laboratory. He was engaged in cancer research. Anyone who
knows these experiments knows that a great deal of technical
skill is required to make crystallization succeed properly. I
was not particularly inclined towards such technical skills
but I nevertheless succeeded one day in creating a crystalliza-
tion. The experience of seeing the crystals radiating out to the
periphery from a central point made a deep impression on me.
I suddenly became aware that a spiritual element forms matter
and can give it direction. This experience might be described
as an ego-experience.

At 21 I also had the wish to undertake a journey by myself.
The opportunity arose of travelling to Argentina. My father
placed great trust in me and my innocence protected me. That
applied very frequently more generally during this time, for
I often came home late as I attended various art schools and
theatre performances with friends from university.

Anthroposophy expanded my horizons immeasurably.
When I was 22 an old anthroposophical doctor from Ham-
burg, Dr Maijen, came to Brazil and gave some lectures on
Goethe. On this occasion I became acquainted with my first
husband, Peter Schmidt. He came from the United States and
was spending his holidays in Brazil. His holidays lasted no

more than three weeks and we used this time intensively to get to know one another. Then he had to return to the States to finish his studies. A lively correspondence ensued. It led to an engagement which we wrote to one another on postcards. My father was not terribly enthusiastic about this step in the beginning, but since he had used a pendulum to find the name Peter for me before I was born, he did see this as in some way destined by fate. The only condition he set was that I should finish my studies. That was no great problem for me since I felt no desire to interrupt my studies. But my fiancé interrupted his studies and did not fully complete them as he had some important reasons for returning to Brazil — one of them being my existence, of course. We married after his arrival although we had become somewhat estranged by the distance. But since my parents wanted to travel to Europe and we were to look after the house we decided to marry immediately. When we look back on that time today we both feel that we should have left ourselves a little more time then, particularly as this was my first love affair.

My first daughter, Aglaia, was born during my studies when I was 23. She was delivered in the university hospital. I was allowed to use the nurses' crèche and thus I was able to breast feed her even while I was at the university. It was a difficult time for me, not being able to fulfil my maternal duties to the full during my studies. We lived with my parents-in-law at the time and there was a great deal of conflict between them and my husband and me.

I received my doctor's diploma at 24 and in the following year I worked as a junior doctor in the department of internal medicine. In the meantime my father was waiting impatiently for me to take over the medical running of the physiotherapy institute. He had already set up a surgery for me there. Thus I was already able to work in my own practice while I was still working at the university.

My second daughter, Solway, was born when I was 25. I felt at that time already that I found medicine very easy. But

*bringing up children and having a family of my own was a new
experience to me. And I had to work at it, bit by bit.*

*When I was 26, my parents-in-law and a number of other
couples founded the Waldorf school in São Paolo. I decided
to become its school doctor. Inwardly I had to face the question how I was to become school doctor in a Waldorf school
if I was not yet acquainted with anthroposophical medicine.
At that moment I decided to write to the then Clinical-
Therapeutic Institute in Arlesheim. I came into contact with
Dr Alexander Leroi, a Portuguese man who worked at the
Institute. My husband and I prepared for a trip to Europe. My
husband went to the company 'Giroflex' in Switzerland, the
parent company of his Brazilian firm, and I went to Arlesheim
with the assistance of a grant from Weleda. There I had the
opportunity to attend a one-month introductory course for
doctors and developed an enthusiasm for eurythmy. I did not
yet understand a great deal of the content of the lectures. But
I liked it very much in Arlesheim and I grew increasingly at
home in this world. My husband, who visited me at weekends,
was astonished at my inner transformation. Once the course
was finished, I worked a further three months at the clinic
with Dr Leroi, and a deep friendship developed between us
which lasted until his death.*

*When I was 27, he came for a visit to Brazil with his wife.
He found our medicine cabinet in our bathroom. Here we kept
the medicines which my husband filled into smaller bottles
at the weekend and then distributed to the patients. On that
occasion we decided to found a 'Weleda' in Brazil. My step-
mother died in the same year. In this year, too, increasing
numbers of European teachers, mainly from Germany, came
to the Brazilian Waldorf school and a lively working group
developed.*

At 28 I had German measles together with my children.

*My husband and I joined anthroposophical working groups
and circles of anthroposophical teachers at the Waldorf
school. It was a phase of many new discoveries in our lives.*

*We had contact with many young people. When I was expect-
ing my third child, Thomas, I had the wish to take a break from
my work. Thus we went to Europe, although I was pregnant,
and on a wonderful tour of Italy.*

*Thomas was born two months after our return. I always
enjoyed the period when I nursed the children for I was able to
concentrate wholly on the child. For the rest of the time I felt a
certain split within me. I had to attend to my family on the one
hand and my medical work on the other. Looking back today,
I believe that I was given too much responsibility at too early
an age. I am thinking of my father's expectation, for example,
that I should be responsible for the institute of physiotherapy. I
was never ill and my only opportunity for staying at home was
during pregnancy and the subsequent nursing period. That is
why I enjoyed that time in particular.*

*The Waldorf school had bought a new plot of land outside
São Paolo and many people who were interested in Waldorf
education moved to the southern part of the city. Conflicts
often arose between the younger teachers from Europe and the
older ones who had lived in Brazil for a long time. Since I was
the school's representative vis-à-vis the government, some
teachers tried to exploit my position for their personal gain.
Because of my lack of experience in relationships, I became
involved in situations which I could not handle. We might say
that there was a Luciferic element in these involvements and I
felt a strongly Luciferic seduction during this time. I was often
in the limelight and many teachers fell in love with me. One
day I suddenly realized that these situations arose because
I radiated a certain aura which provoked the teachers into
behaving in this way. From that time onwards I was able to
handle these things better.*

*In my thirtieth year, when Thomas was seven months old,
my father fell ill from cancer of the thyroid. It was very difficult for him to understand why it was just he, having lived such
a healthy life, who should be struck down by this illness. After
he had undergone surgery and radiation treatment, he went*

to the Ita Wegman Clinic in Arlesheim for nursing care. I was able to be with him for the last two weeks of his life. He died in a special hospital in Basle on Maundy Thursday. I returned to Brazil immediately after his cremation.

We had begun building our own house before that event. At approximately the same time we also bought a plot of land in the mountains. The crisis in the school was increasing. During this time I had a profound meeting with Helmut von Kügelgen who was in Brazil on a visit and was giving lectures. He helped me to gain a better understanding of the confusion at the school and among the teachers on a soul level. This was an encounter which represented a turning point in my spiritual anthroposophical life and which led to an encounter with the Christ being in a new form and meditation. It happened in the middle of my thirty-second year.

After that we travelled to Argentina together. Helmut von Kügelgen held educational lectures and I medical ones. I had important encounters with many people in that time, including Gerhard Jödicke and Willi Woldijk. My husband, too, took part in this new life. I studied Rudolf Steiner's lectures to young people intensively and I wanted to proclaim them to everyone. I had always been engaged in a meditative life. Once I had become acquainted with the anthroposophical literature, I studied Steiner's Christmas and Easter courses for teachers intensively. This broadened my inner, meditative life beyond the purely medical and I tried to gain a more comprehensive understanding of the world.

Relations in the Waldorf school broke down completely and the newly arrived teachers left the school. That was also the time for me to leave the school. I had the feeling that I had done enough there and felt inwardly that my real work lay somewhere else: namely to found an anthroposophical clinic here in São Paolo. My father, too, had in the past supported the idea of starting a clinic. But I felt that the old physiotherapeutic medicine was not my way, but that it was specifically the anthroposophical way which provided me with answers to the questions which I had already asked myself earlier in relation to my mother's behaviour.

My father-in-law now joined my husband's factory. He sold his own business in order to associate himself with the new endeavour. But my husband wondered inwardly: 'Is that my path, or does education here in São Paolo require new teachers?' So we decided to move our whole household and children to Europe for a year or two. Thomas had just turned three at the time. The children were fortunate enough to be able to join classes one and three at the Stuttgart Waldorf school. My husband Peter attended the seminar for Waldorf education and Thomas and I initially stayed at home. Life in Stuttgart was not so simple at first. Our children were noisy like Brazilians and looking after the household was a great burden to me. I often went to the seminar for curative education in Eckwälden near Bad Böll where I enthusiastically studied curative eurythmy with Else Sittel and attended classes in massage and curative painting with Margarethe Hauschka. In Stuttgart itself I learned about special pharmaceutical processes with the old pharmacist Spiess.

I had important meetings with Ernst Lehrs and Mrs Röschel-Lehrs and we had many profound conversations about the anthroposophical path of schooling. There was a small group of doctors in Heumaden near Stuttgart with whom I easily established contact. My soul was filled more and more with the great riches which people gave to me. They exercised an exceptional influence on my medical work and I draw on this source today still. That time in Europe was among the most fruitful in my life.

We had an important encounter with Bernard Lievegoed at Christmas in the Arlesheim group. This encounter was decisive especially for my husband. He had the opportunity to travel to Holland on several occasions in order to become more closely acquainted with Professor Lievegoed's work. My husband recognized that his task lay in adult education within the framework of Mr Lievegoed's work. For us, this time was one of meeting and separation, meeting again and separating again, and each one of us had new and enthusiastic things to report. It was a very fruitful time.

The time in Stuttgart soon came to an end. Our ship, a Belgian freighter, went from Antwerp to Brazil. There were no safety measures on board and Thomas had a fall from one of the decks. He kept being sick for a whole week. When we arrived in São Paolo, a radiography of his head revealed that his skull was cracked in a straight line from front to back. He had to stay in bed for a considerable time longer before he was well again.

We returned from Germany in 1964. In Brazil, the military coup against the communists was just taking place. It happened mainly in São Paolo — not a good time, then, to start something new in Brazil. But our parents-in-law had been pressing for our return because there was not a single doctor at that time who prescribed Weleda medicines. My husband decided to start his social educational work in his company 'Giroflex.' He even thought about setting up an apprentice training scheme. A former kindergarten teacher from São Paolo came to us to devote herself to this work here in Brazil. A handwork teacher from the Stuttgart Waldorf school also joined us. Our new house was near the Waldorf school and developed into a small therapeutic centre. A curative eurythmist from Stuttgart also joined us. Our house became a cultural centre in which small concerts, theatre performances and, above all, the Christmas plays were performed.

We were increasingly taken with the idea of building a clinic — and the idea was reinforced when my husband once found a patient with a high temperature in his bed when he returned home.

I travelled to Argentina once more when I was 35 in order to undertake some medical and educational work at the Waldorf school there.

Our friend Anna Lahusen gave me an interest-free loan to start building work on the clinic. When we returned from

Germany we saw that it did not make sense to continue with my father's institute of physiotherapy. We sold the institute and bought three plots of land with the proceeds which were situated not far from our house. They became the land for the 'Clinica Tobias.' It lay about five minutes away between our house and the school. My husband, Peter, drew up the building plans together with a young engineer. Peter was also occupied with a small social-educational school in his company 'Giroflex.' In addition, he managed the company as well.

At 37½ the foundation stone of the clinic was ready to be laid. It was a spiritual event in which our European friends also participated. Greetings and good wishes came from all over the world and one had the impression that a bright light was streaming into the dodecahedron of the foundation stone.

Our happy family life came to an end at this time. For I had always had the feeling in my life up to that point that everything was easy, that I had great luck and that everything just fell into my lap. I felt that an impulse was beginning to arise in my life. Sometimes I even thought that I should leave home for six months in order to be dependent solely on myself and perhaps live with indigenous people and help them. But the existence of my family meant that I never had the courage to take that step. Now a phase occurred which I consider a negative one in my life, although, looking back on it, it broadened my experience considerably and led to a confrontation with evil. This has taught me over time to develop a tremendous tolerance towards other people. I would not have developed sufficient humility had I not gone through these events myself.

A friendship developed between the people in a village nearby and me. I brought a new cultural impulse to the simple lives of these people, and our children even performed Christmas plays in the small Catholic chapel there.

I became pregnant again shortly after the foundation stone of 'Clinica Tobias' had been laid. I knew that it would be a boy and that he should be called Tiago. The walls of the clinic slowly grew during my pregnancy. My husband devoted a great deal of time to the building during that period; he received little support from me in this task. The birth of Tiago was a great pleasure for all our patients and acquaintances. His name is deeply connected with the place Santiago de Compostela which I only got to know when I was 60.

We intended to establish a home in our house for boys who came from the village mentioned above near our farm. But we only got as far as taking in a five-year-old boy who became like an adopted son. Thus Thomas had another brother to take his attention. I devoted myself completely to nursing my small child again and did not want to work on the clinic which was to be opened soon. Thus its inauguration was delayed and took place in the middle of my thirty-ninth year. I noticed that my life forces were waning a little; at the same time I was faced with two tremendous tasks: bringing up a small child and the work in the clinic. We had found some doctors who were interested in working at the clinic. The clinic was turned into a charity on the day of its inauguration. It was given the name 'Associaçao Beneficiente Tobias.' From the beginning a small community of nurses, masseuses, therapists and some outside doctors formed.

At the age of 42 I had an encounter with a doctor who was working with us and who was a member of the Rosicrucian movement. He held the view that I was a true Rosicrucian and wanted to bring me into his school. I visited the sites there a number of times and had the impression of being in ancient Egypt. During this time I also had a dream in which I went through an Egyptian initiation. Many things about my relationship with this doctor on a personal level became clear to me.

During this time, at about the age of 42, I had the feeling of being in a dark tunnel. I knew that there were certain illuminated moments, but then they disappeared from my consciousness again. I clearly saw the light at the end of the tunnel and what I had to do to get there. My relationship with my husband became more and more difficult. We grew thoroughly apart from one another. My husband was always away

*on trips to Europe and I was busy in the clinic introducing the
other doctors to anthroposophical medicine. At the same time
I was involved in a new friendship in which I was held like in
a trance, and I was unable to do any spiritual and esoteric
work. Outwardly everything took its normal course with various duties, looking after the patients and so on. But inwardly
I felt torn apart, in conflict. On the one hand I had great inner
longing for spiritual work which I had always done in my life,
and on the other hand I felt the impossibility of doing it. I felt
as if I was trapped in a spider's web.*

*In that period we began extension work on the clinic. We
also bought a farm for organic agriculture. Some young people from Europe came to undertake this task and we helped to
create the appropriate social structures there. But it was no
easy task. Often generational conflicts arose. Looking back
to that time, both the younger and older people feel that we
learnt a great deal from this situation and that many things
bore fruit. Our house had gradually turned into a place where
people could come and stay at any time — no matter from
where they had arrived. This, of course, seriously affected the
privacy of our family life.*

*Once my husband began with his social-educational work in
the company I began to develop an interest in it as well, which I
had not done before. I began to work there with anthroposophical medicine and after a while I became the company doctor
and went there twice a week. I was particularly interested in
the affairs of the workers at that time. We created meaningful
Christmas celebrations and put on plays. A kindergarten was
started as well. All of this made a significant contribution to the
cultural enrichment of the factory. My life was thus developing
in three areas: in the social-educational work in my husband's
factory, in the Tobias Clinic and in our family life.*

*I never stopped trying to spend our holidays mostly with the
children. We went on major trips through Brazil at this time.
We visited indigenous settlements, went on boat trips and took
the train to Bolivia and Peru. We undertook a major journey*

to the north-eastern part of Brazil with Thomas, Solway and
one friend each in which we drove along the whole coast to
Fortaleza.

My husband and I felt a certain impotence. We no longer
really knew how to conduct our life together.

The clinic and the number of patients was growing. In addition, young medical students and doctors came who wanted to
find out about anthroposophical medicine and to have training
from us. We started regular training courses in anthroposophical medicine for them.

We always had to organize donations and encourage people to help. A Mr D turned up one day who wanted to help
in some way but was unable to do so financially. We needed
someone who was able to take on the social-education work
here in Brazil. So this gentleman, who was anyway looking for
a new field of work, decided to go and be trained. A year later
he went to Europe for training at NPI (Netherlands Pedagogi-
cal Institute). He returned to Brazil at the end of his training. I
organized a conference together with Mr D, a Waldorf teacher
and a farmer on the subject 'Introduction to practical anthroposophical work.' I was 45 at the time. The enlarged clinic
meant that it was necessary to search for new directions. The
second seven-year-period, which the institution had by now
entered, clearly made itself felt and new standards, working
methods, etc. had to be introduced. We invited Mr D for this
purpose. He was to advise us on these questions. He arrived in
our library with large rolls of paper and a black briefcase. An
argument arose between us about wasting paper and ecological awareness. This conflict situation had to be resolved and
so we had a first personal talk with the assistance of a third
person. But the talk did not lead to any outcome and we tried it
later once more on our own. My husband was in Europe again
at this time. I invited Mr D to see a play, a peasant Christmas
play from the north-east of Brazil. This visit to the theatre
turned into a true encounter between us. In order to get to
know one another better, we decided to go to the sea for a day

*and tell each other our lifestories. We were both certain that
no relationship other than marriage came into question for us.
And Mr D became Daniel, my second husband.*

*Shortly before Peter, my first husband, went to Europe,
he went on a trip with me to the sea in the south and he had
the impression that this was his last journey with me. He was
not able to explain his feeling. But my encounter with Mr D
confirmed his premonition. I told Peter about our new situation during his European visit. He became acquainted with
his new, second wife during this period while he was at the
Clinical-Therapeutic Institute in Arlesheim. We clarified our
situation after Peter's return and decided on divorce.*

*Thus a new life began for me. Peter, with whom I have a
very strong and deeply inward spiritual relationship to this
day, contributed and helped very intensively to ensure that
our separation did not affect our general work in the various
areas, particularly the clinic. I always felt the relationship with
my husband to be of a paternal nature and I still go to him for
advice. But in my soul I had the feeling from my mid-twenties
onwards that I would meet someone else who was important
to me. And I had always searched for that person. This feeling
disappeared completely after my meeting with Daniel.*

*Looking back, I can say that the meeting with my second
husband uncovered many new elements in me to which I was
already predisposed. Through Peter I had come into contact
with social-educational issues and the work of Professor
Lievegoed. This element was strengthened further through the
relationship with Daniel. We decided to start lifestory seminars after Daniel's friend, Helmuth J. ten Siethoff, had been
to stay here in Brazil and encouraged us to unite our forces
— Daniel as management consultant and I as doctor. Here we
have found a joint field of work which has carried on developing over the years.*

*My first husband, Peter, asked his future second wife to
come from Germany and she took loving care of Tiago's
upbringing. Thus I was able to continue my work at the clinic*

*and the seminars on anthroposophical medicine. There was
much to do.*

*After two years in which we lived near the clinic and my
old house, we had the opportunity to sell my last inheritance,
a house by the sea. We acquired a rather large site outside
São Paolo with the proceeds. We planned to build a house for
ourselves here later and perhaps gradually to develop a new
site for our work. 'Artemisia' was created on this property
over the years: our present lifestory centre and holiday home.*

*I had an important experience when the clinic had been
in existence precisely seven years. I had to give a speech at
the clinic. I was very confused and did not know exactly how
to approach it. I went for a rhythmical massage and was still
lying on the massage table when I felt a great being over the
clinic. I was convinced that this being was Ita Wegman. From
this moment onwards I knew what I was going to say in my
speech at the clinic. And I decided to study Ita Wegman's and
Rudolf Steiner's path of destiny. One or two years later, once
my inner soul life had calmed down, I was able to realize that
by joining the Easter circle of anthroposophical doctors which
meets annually in Arlesheim. From then on I occupied myself
with this task.*

*When I was 49, Daniel and I had the opportunity to free
ourselves somewhat from our work here. We travelled to England for five months and visited the 'Centre of Social Development.' We also went on a wonderful trip to Ireland and visited
Agathe and Norbert Glas. Agathe told us much about the pixies. When we drove to southern Ireland we camped near a wild
burn where we did not see another person the whole day long.
There Daniel experienced the pixies — it was the crowning
moment of our trip!*

*I was now entering my seventh seven-year-period and felt
that there had to be a change in my life. I was very attentive
and open to the questions and tasks which I encountered
from outside. On the one hand there were the young medical
students who were demanding training and continuously new*

courses; Dr Otto Wolff was a great help in this. But on the other hand there were also young people from other professions, such as psychologists and social educationalists. We therefore decided, together with Alexander and Johanna Bos, to institute social-education seminars as well as the medical courses. In 1981 it became necessary to look for a new building to house all these seminars. Thus a new training centre came into existence with the assistance of 'Associaçao Tobias.' Social educationalists could be trained here and advanced medical training seminars held, as well as art therapy seminars in the last three years. We called this centre 'Centro Paulus.' We transferred the lifestory courses from the Tobias Clinic to the new building for a transitional period. But this was not the right solution for our lifestory courses in the long term. In addition, we needed a place where our patients from the clinic could recuperate. Thus we decided to donate 'Artemisia' to the Tobias association, extend the buildings and set up a centre for lifestory courses, for cleansing and dietary as well as recuperative visits by stressed patients. 'Artemisia' has been in existence for nine years. It is situated approximately three quarters of an hour away from the Tobias Clinic and is still surrounded by tropical forest — even if civilization is encroaching ever closer. 'Artemisia' turned into a place in which people feel comfortable, are able to stand back from the rush and commune with nature.

Another task with which I was faced in my eighth seven-year-period was connected with the request to describe nutrition from an anthroposophical perspective in a book about alternative nutrition. The chapter was to be no longer than 30 pages, but as I had written almost a whole book, I published it in its own right. It is called New Ways of Nutrition *and comprises four volumes. They have provided a stimulus for many people to pursue nutritional methods based on anthroposophy. I felt the strong involvement of my father as I was writing the book. A further book about the zodiac appeared three years later.*

In the meantime, Daniel and I have gone through several crises. Daniel gave up his consultancy work for several years and worked intensively in the 'Associaçao Beneficiente Tobias' and particularly in the management of the clinic. He returned to his consultancy work only five years ago.

During this time we experienced how difficult it can be if one's own house — or rather, one room and bathroom — are directly adjacent to one's place of work when there are continuous lifestory seminars which frequently keep one occupied from seven in the morning until ten at night. We also often work at the weekends, since our patients have more time at the weekend than during the week. Thus we have not really had a private home of our own to live in since then. Daniel finally moved into a small house and six years ago we were in a position to build our own house on the site.

We maintained our holiday pattern. Once a year we took one month long holiday. Two years ago we had a car crash at the start of our holiday in which I broke two vertebra. I lay on the ground for one-and-a-half hours and did not really know what had happened. My 'organ of fate,' the thorax, had been injured again. In the ambulance I had the same feelings as at nine when I was run over by the car.

I did not experience any great changes in the transition phase at 56 — lunar node and start of a new seven-year-period. But earlier, when I was 54 — a mirror image of the age of nine — I almost drowned.

In the transition to my ninth seven-year-period it was clear to me that I had to approach my tasks in a new way. It took one or two years for me to realize that the new tasks had developed quite by themselves with my visits to Europe. Here in Europe I began with lifestory work for cancer patients at the Lukas Clinic in Switzerland and, from 1989 onwards, I held courses in Switzerland, Germany, Spain and Portugal for different kinds of therapists who wanted to become involved in lifestory work. I believe those were the new colours for the ninth seven-year-period.

*The changes were further reaching when I turned 60 —
the second Saturn cycle was coming to an end and a new one
was beginning. It was a great gift for me to be cared for in
the Tobias Clinic for four weeks after my car crash. I had
many conversations and refreshed old relationships. When I
look back on the crash today and feel completely recovered,
I can only marvel at the wisdom of fate. It always provided
me with the right things; here, too, it created a conclusion
to the second Saturn phase in which death and resurrection
appeared in my life again. The crash taught me once again
the importance of people having an aim in life. It is the great
secret of development that we should always set ourselves
new objectives.*

*When I lay in bed after the crash, unable to move, my
sole aim was to lift my head or turn on my side so that I
could clean my teeth and eat by myself. Once I had achieved
that, my aim was gradually to sit upright, read a little, be
independent. The next aim was to have a new corset made
and to learn to walk in it. They were very small, immediate objectives, which broadened out as my condition slowly
improved. During that time I also experienced the presence
of two deceased people who had had a close connection to
the clinic — one of my patients and the author of the 'Letter
from a twenty-one-year-old' reproduced on page 58. I was
an example to them of how to rebuild one's body, in my case
the vertebrae. Every day these deceased people were present
at my sickbed.*

*One thing which caused me great problems was that my
head was unable to be creative while my legs were not working. For example, it was quite impossible to write a book in
bed. I am certain that many new opportunities will come from
this situation in future.*

*My husband, Daniel, and I were able to deepen our rela-
tionship. It is now in its seventeenth year.*

*Looking back on my lifestory, I have discovered an impor-
tant law in the middle phases. Between 21 and 28 I worked*

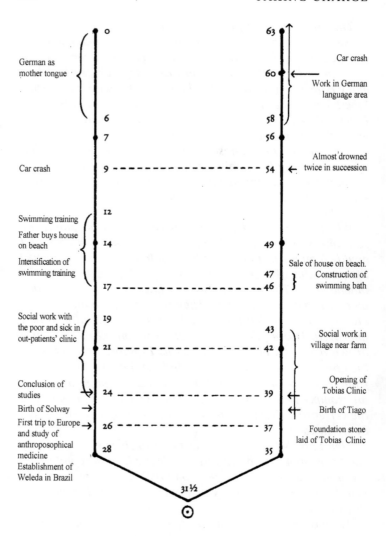

Figure 20. Some mirror images in my biography.

hard at acquiring a knowledge of anthroposophical medicine. Between 28 and 35, mainly during my stay in Germany from 32 to 34, I deepened it with the artistic element — with rhythmical massage, curative eurythmy, art therapy (painting) and the observation of art. Finally, between 35 and 42 the laying of the foundation stone and inauguration of the clinic took place. The path from the head to the deed via the heart became visible to me.

This process was repeated in a similar form in my work in social-education, leading to my lifestory work: learning (from 42 to 49), practice (from 49 to 56) and realization of the impulse and founding of a centre for the work ('Artemisia') in my fifty-fourth year.

Some mirror images can be seen in Figure 20 in which my thirty-second year provides the mid-point. There is little that emerges in my lifestory by way of mirror images if we take 21 as the mid-point. We can see from my lifestory (and also from those of other people) that there are something like 'years of anticipation' which are sometimes even mirrored. We might describe them as 'pregnant years' of a kind. Thus for example:

Birth of Solway 24–26.　　　　*37–39 Birth of Tiago*

Waiting for the trip to Arlesheim — and learning about anthroposophical medicine.

Waiting for the opening of the clinic: implementation of anthroposophical medicine.

17–18　　　　　　　　　　*45–46*

Intensive preparatory year for university.

New, intense love for Daniel; concentrated study of Rudolf Steiner's lecture cycles.

My relationships with other people were very chaotic in the first half of the fifth seven-year-period (the time when I was working as a school doctor). Then, between the ages of 31 and 32, a development occurred which led to my relationships with other people being imbued with a Christian spirit. My European trip in the second half of this seven-year-period led to new, key relationships which were decisive for my subsequent professional activity.

As far as my work is concerned, I had my own practice for fourteen years (from 25 to 39). In addition, I worked for six years as a school doctor and in my father's institute, two years in Europe, and a further six years at home in the therapeutic institute. This was followed by fourteen years at the Tobias Clinic, during seven of which I carried sole responsibility for the enterprise with the administrative assistance of my husband, and a further seven years as part of a group of people carrying responsibility for the clinic. My second husband, Daniel, also worked intensively in this group. Two years later, I had completely disengaged myself from this group. In 'Artemisia' too — I began my work there at 53 — a 'circle of supporters' formed after seven years. My husband, Daniel, began giving courses to support companies in their development. The seven-year-rhythm is apparent here as well, then.

I am active in the medical field to the present day. The patients come to 'Artemisia' and I am able to make available to them my innate skill, the ability to heal which has always lived in me, not only by prescribing medicines, but also through the lifestory seminars which I run.

São Paolo, May 1992

Acknowledgments

Juan Ramón Jiménez: 'Ich bin nich ich' from *Herz stirb oder singe. Gedichte*. Spanish and German. Selected and translated by Hans Leopold Davi. © 1977 Diogenes Verlag AG, Zurich. English translation by Christian von Arnim.

Vaclav Hável from *Am Anfang war das Wort. Essays.* © 1990 Rowohlt Verlag, Reinbek. English translation by Christian von Arnim.

Hermann Hesse: 'Stufen' from *Gesammelte Werke*, Vol. 1. © 1970 Suhrkamp Verlag, Frankfurt am Main. English translation by Christian von Arnim.

Rudolf Steiner: All rights to Rudolf Steiner's texts reside with the Rudolf Steiner Nachlassverwaltung, Dornach, Switzerland. English translations by Christian von Arnim except 'The wishes of the soul are springing' from *Verses and Meditations*, Anthroposophical Publishing Co., London 1961.

Rudolf Meyer: © Verlag Urachhaus, Stuttgart. English translation by Christian von Arnim.

Bibliography

Aschenbrenner, Michael, *Tierkreis und Menschenwesen*, Dornach 1972.

Flensburger Hefte No. 31, Biographiearbeit.

Fromm, Erich, *Die Kunst des Liebens*, Frankfurt/Main, Berlin 1992.

——, *Haben oder Sein. Die seelischen Grundlagen einer neuen Gesellschaft*, München 1991.

Gammnitz, Gisela, *Vom Altwerden. Materialiensammlung aus der Rudolf Steiner Gesamtausgabe*, Dornach 1987.

Glas, Norbert, *Frühe Kindheit*, Stuttgart 1957.

——, *Gefährdung und Heilung der Sinne*, Stuttgart 1984.

——, *Jugendzeit und mittleres Alter*, Stuttgart 1960.

——, *The Fulfillment of Old Age*, Anthroposophic Press, New York.

Goethe, Johann Wolfgang, *The Green Snake and the Beautiful Lily*, Temple Lodge Press, London.

Grimm, *The Complete Grimms' Tales for Young and Old*, Doubleday, New York 1977, and Gollancz, London 1978.

Hahn, Herbert, *Der Lebenslauf als Kunstwerk*, Stuttgart 1966.

Heuwold, Horst, *Den Faden wieder aufnehmen*, Stuttgart 1989.

Holtzapfel, Walter, *Auf dem Weg zum Hygienischen Okkultismus*, Dornach 1988.

Jocelyn, Beredene, *Cosmic Citizens*.

Julius, Frits H., *The Imagery of the Zodiac*, Floris Books, Edinburgh 1994.

Jung, C.G., Marie L. von Franz (eds.), *Man and his Symbols*, Aldus Books, London 1964.

——, *Collected Works, Vol. 8*. Routledge & Kegan Paul, London.

König, Karl, *Brothers and Sisters*, Floris Books, Edinburgh 1993.

——, *The Human Soul*, Floris Books, Edinburgh 1993.

Lauenstein, Dieter, *Biblical Rhythms in Human Biography*, Floris Books, Edinburgh 1983.

Lauer, H. Erhard, *Der menschliche Lebenslauf*, Freiburg 1952.

Lebenshilfen Vol.2, Lebenslauf. *Das Ich als geistige Wirklichkeit*, Stuttgart 1989.

Levinson, Daniel J., *The Seasons of a Man's Life*, New York 1979.

Lewis, Spencer, *Self Mastery and Fate with the Cycles of Life*, California 1975.

Lievegoed, Bernard, *Phases of Childhood*, Floris Books, Edinburgh, 1997.

——, *Man on the Threshold*, Hawthorn Press, Stroud.

——, *Phases*, Rudolf Steiner Press , London.

Nordmeyer, Barbara, *Lebenskrisen und ihre Bewältigung*, Stuttgart 1982.

O'Neill, Gisela and George, *The Human Life*, Mercury Press, New York.

Sheehy, Gail, *Pathfinders*, New York 1981.

——, *Predictable Crises of Adult Life*, New York 1976.

Steiner, Rudolf, *Karmic Relationships*, Vols. I–VI, Rudolf Steiner Press, London.

——, *The Effects of Spiritual Development (CW145)*, Rudolf Steiner Press, UK 1978.

——, *How to Know Higher Worlds*, Anthroposophic Press, New York.

——, *An Outline of Occult Science*, Anthroposophic Press, New York 1989.

——, *Metamorphoses of the Soul, Vols. 1 and 2*, Rudolf Steiner Press London.

——, *Manifestations of Karma*, Anthroposophic Press, New York 1983.

——, *Reincarnation and Karma*, Anthroposophic Press, New York.

——, 'Soziale und antisoziale Triebe im Menschen,' Lecture of 12 December 1918, in *Die soziale Grundforderung unserer Zeit — In geänderter Zeitlage*, GA 186, Dornach 1988.

——, *Theosophy*, Rudolf Steiner Press, London 1970.

——, *Vom Lebenslauf des Menschen*, twelve lectures, Stuttgart 1991.

Treichler, Rudolf, *Metamorphosen im Lebenslauf*, Dornach 1984.

——, Soulways, Hawthorn Press, Stroud.

Vreede, Elisabeth, *Anthroposophie und Astronomie*, Freiburg 1954.

Zeylmans van Emmichoven, F. Willem, *Die menschliche Seele*, Basel 1979.

Floris Books

For news on all our **latest books**,
and to receive **exclusive discounts**,
join our mailing list at:

florisbooks.co.uk

Plus subscribers get a FREE book
with every online order!

We will never pass your details to anyone else.